With Fabric & Thread

With Fabric & Thread

More Than 20 Inspired Quilting &
Sewing Patterns

Joanna Figueroa

WILEY

John Wiley & Sons, Inc.

Credits

Senior Editor
Roxane Cerda

Project Editor
Charlotte Kughen,
The Wordsmithery LLC

Editorial Manager
Christina Stambaugh

Vice President and Publisher
Cindy Kitchel

Vice President and Executive Publisher
Kathy Nebenhaus

Interior Design
Lissa Auciello-Brogan

Illustrators
Ronda David-Burroughs
Rashell Smith
Cheryl Grubbs

Cover Design
Wendy Mount

Photography
Joanna Figueroa, assisted by Camille Roskelley

To my Figs, big and little. I couldn't even imagine this whole adventure without all four of you in it every day.

Acknowledgments

First I want to thank all the wonderful sewers and quilters who have added their work and expertise to the creation of the projects in this book. You all know that I literally couldn't do it without you, nor would I want to. Working together with all of you is a blessing and a joy! Thank you for all of your work and support of Fig Tree over the years.

Cheryl, I have learned so much from you since that first Monday morning you came to sew in the studio. Your sewing expertise is a refreshing joy for me, and your life stories are something I look forward to each week. You have taught me more than you will ever know and have become our "pretend grandma" in the process!

Sherri (www.aquiltinglife.blogspot.com) and Valerie, your work on the quilts in this book is as amazing as all of your work always is. Both of you never cease to amaze me with your speed, accuracy, and helpful spirit whenever I have a deadline! Thank you both for your dedication and loyalty to me over the years. I so wish you both lived closer.

Diana (QuiltedGrammy@aol.com): You know this to be true because I have told you this a hundred times: My quilts are just not the same without your amazing quilting work to finish them into the beauties that they now are. Your work on each and every single quilt and quilted item in this book does not go unnoticed! I will always think of you as "my quilter". All mine. Thank you!

A huge thank you goes out to MODA fabrics and especially to Mark, Cheryl, and Lissa for your support of all of my endeavors, fabric ideas and for your amazing marketing and business help over the years. On a practical note, I am so grateful for all of the amazing fabric that is the reason for most of the projects in this book. MODA rocks!

I also want to thank Roxane, my editor, for attending my class at the Creative Connection, hosting that first fun dinner out, and believing in the idea of this book. Even through maternity leave and dozens of sleepless nights you have been a wonderful support and help throughout the trickiest portions of making this book come together. Thank you for all your calmness, wisdom, and support!

A special thank you also to Charlotte, and anyone else on the design and editing team, who has had to put up with my questions, my scribbles, my notes, and my emails. You have turned a thousand scraps of paper and fabric into a wonderful book.

John Wiley & Sons would like to thank the following people for their invaluable help in testing projects in this book prior to publication:

- Kristy Smith of Hopeful Threads
- Jennifer Latourette
- Mary Jo Larsen
- Annebelle Gardner
- Mary Jaracyz
- Garilyn Sponseller

pg. 167

pg. 84

pg. 127

pg. 136

pg. 131

pg. 89

pg. 94

pg. 74

pg. 80

pg. 157

pg. 102

pg. 171

pg. 153

pg. 144

pg. 148

pg. 120

pg. 162

pg. 113

Introduction

WELCOME!

As I work on the final edits of this manuscript, I find my mind turning more and more to you, the reader. I find that I am daydreaming about who you might be and what you will find most useful and inspirational in these pages. As I wind down my journey of writing this book, you might just be starting out on yours. Certainly you are just beginning the journey of working through this particular book, and I can't help but wonder what part it will play in your story. Try as I might to focus on the technical aspects of making sure these pages are error free, I find myself imagining what you will think of while you are reading. I wonder what your favorite projects might be, hoping that some of my favorites will be yours as well. As an author, it is a wonderful and scary journey to write down all that you think others might want to know about your process and your craft. It is truly an adventure that, although I have done many times before, stretches and teaches me new things about myself and my work each time I do it. For me, I feel like there is always something else to add and something else to share but as I reflect on what else I could possibly add, I thought of a story that my mom recently reminded me about. Given that I wasn't sure exactly where in the book it might find its "fit," I decided to share it with you here, at the very beginning.

The very first time I visited the United States, and thus found myself on a very long trans-Atlantic flight, I was three and a half years old. Suffice it to say that I was a bubbly and extroverted little girl who wanted nothing to do with sitting in a plane seat for hours at a time. As the story goes, my mom searched frantically for something to occupy my time. Finding nothing better, she handed me a small bag of mismatched buttons and a needle and thread and sent me on my way. What happened next entertained not only me but the entire crew and all the passengers I could get my hands on. For the next five hours, I meticulously sewed buttons to the pant legs and sleeves of any aisle customers who would give me the time of day. I intently tried to use every last button in my little bag. Apparently, no one objected, and I was mesmerized and entranced by the process. Before I knew it, the plane flight was over and all of my neighbors had more buttons on their clothes than they had started off with! A sewer might well have been born that day.

It would be a long time before I would remember that story, and I am not quite sure exactly why I wanted to share it with you here. I thought at the very least it would give you one more insight into how much our lives can come full circle without our slightest knowledge or planning. Who knows where you started out and where you might land. In some small way, I hope to be a part of that journey for you as you work through the pages of this book.

Happy sewing,
Joanna

My Story

My Personal and Creative Journey

As we reach adulthood, choose our careers, and start down the paths that the rest of our lives will take, many of us look back to see if there were markers or milestones along the way that pointed us in a particular direction. We wonder if we have made the right choices and also wonder how we arrived at the life that we now live. Whether we know it at the time or not, many of us have those moments that we can point to that, in looking back, were clear markers of our futures. For most of us it was a mix of the natural loves of our lives, the circumstances we found ourselves in, and decisions that we made. I believe that we are all a mix of those things in one way or another. For me, looking back, my path started when I was a little girl in a yellow dress.

The Little Girl in the Yellow Dress

Today if I sit and close my eyes I can still see myself, two simple braids affixed permanently to the sides of my head, wearing my favorite canary yellow sundress with the five rainbow stripes running along the bottom hem. I felt like I could do anything in that dress, and I would have worn it every day if my mom had let me. Somehow on this particular morning, my yellow dress and I managed to go undetected for most of the morning, and by the afternoon we had painted an entire collection of "masterpieces" with my favorite palette of tempera paints. In my memory, my dress remained more or less intact.

I hung all the paintings up on our backyard clothesline and started to make plans for my first business venture. After all, I had my yellow dress on, and I could not fail. Pretty soon I was knocking on every door in our quiet little neighborhood, regaling those who answered with stories of my art. I was convinced that each neighbor would want and need one of my paintings! I guess I must have been quite persuasive because I finished the afternoon with more money than I had ever earned, and a little mustard seed tucked deep inside my soul. I could make art, and I could sell it. People would buy it. That day would become a milestone for me.

Growing Up Entrepreneurial

My drive to make and sell certainly did not start with me, nor was it really that unexpected in our household. Having emigrated from Poland in 1975 under some rather unusual circumstances, my family settled in the United States with very little. My dad brought with him a few thousand dollars, a plan to start a business, and a drive to make a place for us in this new place. And he did. There wasn't a time that I can remember when my sister and I weren't required to do some kind of task for the business before we were allowed to go out and play. I think my favorite memory from my early teens is when we had a quota of shampoo bottles to fill for my dad's new hair care company before we could go out and play in the neighborhood. Boy, did we resent that quota, but we sure did learn the value of hard work and commitment.

A Drive to Create

As I grew up through the years I tried and dabbled in every form of art imaginable. And almost always I tried to sell what I made. Somehow the two were often combined. It was as if the process or the loop wasn't closed for me until the artwork had found a home with an appreciative owner. I fell in love with clay and then with jewelry making. I pursued watercolors and a bit of sculpture. I did macramé and dried flower arrangements. I made homemade soaps and potpourri. I adored playing with typography. I played with printmaking and papermaking. I studied graphic design. Although my parents had supported me in my childhood endeavors, they didn't see art as a viable career option, so I pursued the political sciences, teaching, and later theology and urban studies in my search for what I was going to do when I grew up. Regardless of what I was studying, however, I always felt compelled to create on the side. It almost didn't matter what I was creating. The need to create and to work with my hands was unmistakable as a thread throughout my younger years. Well before I began to realize that it would be the path I was meant to take, I knew that I had to be making something to be content.

My Quilting and Sewing Journey

Even though art was clearly always a part of who I was, fabric was something that I discovered much later on in my journey. It certainly wasn't something that I went looking for. Instead it was almost like it found me by accident. Quilts in particular, as well as many other vintage textiles, had always fascinated me, but it was definitely a fascination from afar. I never imagined that my art would turn to textiles in such a dramatic and complete way.

Falling in Love with Vintage Quilts

As an artist and a crafty person for years, there was something about vintage quilts that naturally drew me to them. I could never identify what exactly it was, but there was something about that perfect blending of something beautiful and something useful that appealed to all parts of who I was and wanted to be. I will never forget the Saturday I was out browsing garage sales near the very first apartment I had with my husband. I happened upon a little yard sale where I discovered my first quilt. It was a baby-sized quilt in a wishbone pattern (which is a wishbone shape made out of many small pieces, kind of like a less-complicated double wedding ring pattern) on a bright bubblegum-pink background. It was a tiny 1930s quilt tied with bright red thread in colors that I would never have pictured myself being drawn to at the time. Yet I fell in love with it instantly and

calmly asked the yard sale owner what she wanted for this "blanket." She took a second to glance at it and told me that I could have it for seven dollars. I worked hard to hide my glee, paid her the money before she could realize that it was worth a lot more, and drove away as fast as I could, feeling the whole time like I had just struck it rich. That was the first of my many quilt finds and rescues from garage sales, flea markets, and antique shops. It was also the first tangible item of my love affair with quilting. I was 25 at the time, and other than stitching a few doll clothes or mending some socks, I had never sewn a day in my adult life.

Self-Taught Beginnings

Soon after the "Wishbone Quilt Incident," as I refer to it now, I happened to walk into a small quilt shop in an indoor shopping mall in my hometown. I must have walked by it a thousand times, but this time I actually walked in, inspired by my newly found vintage acquisition. I signed up for a drop-in quilt class and assumed that meant that I would drop in and someone would teach me something. Instead it was merely a warm seat in a shop with a lot

of fabric to choose from. I bought a machine, chose some fabrics that appealed to me and proceeded to teach myself how to quilt from the books in the store. Once in a while someone would look over my shoulder and make a suggestion or a comment, but mostly I read voraciously and started to quilt. That Christmas, I made quilts as gifts for several of my closest friends and my sister, and I was hooked. I had never experienced the same kind of coming-home feeling in any of my other craft or art pursuits. There was something about working with the fabric that was unlike any other art I had ever worked on. I could choose a palette with the fabrics—each fabric bringing its own life and voice of print and scale—and I could create something that was beautiful and useful at the same time. The colors would sing as they came together in the quilt, and I was mesmerized and completely taken in by the process! In my opinion, there is no other art form that can bring so much pattern, color, and style to our lives and yet still be so functional, utilitarian, and useful as quilting.

A Quilter Who Was Afraid to Sew

And so I became a quilter. I learned everything I could about the art, from its history to its most traditional blocks to the modern interpretations that many quilters were working on. I read about quilting; I stalked my local quilt shops; and I sewed whenever I had extra time. For many years after that, I didn't see myself doing anything else. I certainly did not consider myself a sewer. In all those years I never considered sewing something to wear. I was simply a quilter. I was accurate and my quilts laid flat. That was all I cared about, and all I thought I could do. Anything three-dimensional was beyond my scope. It sounds silly writing it down now, but that is absolutely how I felt then.

In my years in the fabric industry I have heard many talented designers on both sides of the spectrum repeat this comment over and over, and I am sure that I will hear it again. Depending on which side of this glorious world of textiles we come from, we are terrified of exploring or even entering the other side. Just at the last Quilt Market, which is the biannual trade show for our industry, I was chatting with a very talented and prolific quilt pattern designer. When presented with the opportunity to make a completely basic, flat bag for herself, she looked me straight in the eyes and said with the most serious expression, "Oh, Joanna, I could never make a bag. I only know how to sew a flat quilt." I chuckled at her comment, assured her that she could do it, and remembered that only a few years before I would have said the same thing.

In fact, a few years before I *did* say the same exact thing when I was talking about sewing children's clothes with the seamstress who works with me and has been sewing for 35 years. It was her turn to chuckle as she proceeded to put down the quilt she was working on and started to show me this other world that felt so intimidating. Since then I have slowly started to learn to sew. I love to say that! Even though I have been quilting for more than a decade and I run a sewing business, I am just now learning to sew. It is a completely different world in some ways and a close cousin in others. I definitely approach sewing with a quilter's eye and experience, and I often find myself doing things quite differently than someone who started her journey by sewing garments. If you come from the quilting world, it is a journey that I hope you will take with me. If you are a garment sewer, and are dabbling in quilting for the first time, I hope you will work toward me from the opposite direction!

From Quilter to Designer

As a new quilter and an almost immediate fabric addict, my love affair with textiles seemed to know no bounds. The path that opened up in front of me seems to make perfect sense now, when looking back, but at the time it felt like a huge world that I knew very little about. I took it all one step at a time and each new endeavor led me, like Alice, further and further down the rabbit hole!

The Path from Teacher to Designer to Career

Almost as soon as the quilting bug hit me, I started doodling my own ideas. I didn't really pursue creating anything from them, but doodle I did. I filled notebook after notebook of what would later become my first quilt patterns. In the meantime, I felt compelled to sew. It's a funny thing to say out loud, but I felt an almost obsessive need to create blocks and piece them together into quilts. I would stay up all night to finish a quilt that had no deadline! Meanwhile my husband and I relocated to the San Francisco Bay Area, and I found a local quilt shop, Thimblecreek, which would quickly become my home away from home. I didn't know it at the time, but that shop would be the fertile ground that I needed to continue to grow in my craft.

At first I took every class I could, and I became a regular fixture at the store. Soon, however, there weren't any more classes to take and I started working at the shop to help support my fabric habit. My stash had grown to giant proportions, and even though my studio at the time was one side of my son's nursery and my sewing area was the dining room table, I loved what I was doing. I immediately found that my favorite part of working at the shop was choosing fabric palettes for customers' projects. I could literally do it all day long. Something that was hard for so many people seemed to come easily and naturally for me. Without knowing it, I was starting to create my own fabric "collections" in my head as I worked to serve our customers.

Working turned into teaching, which turned into pattern design in a whirlwind of activity. Soon I found myself with more than a dozen original designs that I had created for my classes. The idea that this could be a "real" business started to take shape. With a nursing infant on my lap, what else would I possibly want to do with all that non-existent extra time I had? Looking back, it must have been all those sleepless nights that made me think that I should do this! I could fill a whole book with the events that transpired next to get my business started, but suffice it to say that I had never worked so hard in my life and I had never had so much satisfaction in what I was doing. Fig Tree & Co. was officially born as was my second child. Life was full.

In the Right Place at the Right Time

As a new business owner in the fabric industry, I began to attend our industry's trade show, the International Quilt Market, each spring and fall. It was a great time of getting to know my store customers, building relationships with distributors, finding suppliers for our growing needs, and getting to know the industry in general. As a pattern business with a new, fresh look, our products quickly caught the eye of MODA fabrics, the largest and most well-respected fabric company in our industry. This is one of those serendipitous moments that I am asked about often. I wish I had a better strategic business story to tell, but the truth is that in that moment, I found myself at the right place at the right time. MODA had noticed us, and we had certainly noticed them. In fact, working with MODA was one of those seemingly unattainable goals that I had written down in our business plan as something to work toward. I agreed to create our first fabric line in two weeks' time, although I didn't have a clue how I was going to accomplish it. Let's just say that it was a steep learning curve and a sleepless two weeks!

Today I am working on fabric collection number 22 for MODA, and I have seriously lost count of the quilting and sewing patterns I have produced over the years. I think we might be reaching 200! Today, Fig Tree & Co. works on several different product lines and utilizes our entire family in our business endeavors. Although I could have never pictured myself here when I first started out, I'm not sure I could have planned out a better outcome if I had tried. I can't wait to see where we might go next. I hope you will join me!

Chapter 2

Basics of Quiltmaking

As we start on the journey of this book together, I hope to first take you through some of the basics of quiltmaking. Not an exhaustive list, mind you, but enough to get you familiar with the terms and methods and hopefully enough to entice you along to your first project. The main reason we are starting here is because this is where I started. My basics were all learned while quilting, mostly teaching myself as I went along. I will never forget the making of my first quilt, mostly learning by doing it wrong first. It had so many errors and mistakes that I wasn't even sure I was going to be able to assemble it. I will never part with that quilt and, although I don't think that I will ever show it to anyone, I do know that I will always keep it as both an example of how much I have learned as well as to remind myself that I can do anything I set my mind to.

I believe that you can, too. And as I like to say to my beginning students any time I teach a class, "If you can sew a straight line, you can learn to quilt."

The Basic Terms We Use

¼" Seam Allowance

At the core of all quilt making is the dreaded ¼" seam allowance. If you are able to practice and master the ¼" seam as you sew, your quilts will come together easily and beautifully. Now, please don't get me wrong; you can sew with all kinds of improvisational, "wonky," "modern" methods without using a ¼" seam and still have absolutely beautiful designs and creations. But if you want to create quilts where the pieces come together like they do in the instructions, your blocks match one another, and you don't have to struggle and work to get them to join and become a quilt, you need to practice and master coming as close as you can to a ¼" seam allowance. The simplest ways to do this are to purchase a ¼" seam foot for your machine or to place blue painter's tape on your machine to indicate exactly where the ¼" line is when measured from the point where your needle goes into the fabric. Practice definitely makes perfect in this situation, so plan on a lot of practice!

> **NOTE:** There is something that I would like to add about the ¼" seam allowance to those of you who are just starting out or, perhaps more importantly, to those of you who have a few quilts "under your belt." In many a quilting situation, it is not actually the accuracy of the ¼" seam allowance that is so important. Rather it is most important that you are consistent to yourself! What this means is that in many patterns that don't have to match up to a predetermined sashing or another block, it is more important that all the seams are the same than whether or not they are ¼". Many patterns do not apply to this rule and as you quilt you will begin to see and understand which ones do and which ones don't. Just remember that consistency is huge in quilting!

Squaring Up

Regardless of whether you are working on a quilt block that is contemporary or traditional, the process of squaring up is often important. What this means is that often when you are done with a group of blocks for a quilt, they might not all be exactly the same size. Due to fabric stretching or sewer error, the blocks can sometimes be as different as ¼" in size. The best way to ensure that you are able to put the blocks together in a pleasing way is to find the average of your blocks and "square up" any of the wayward blocks to match the average. Sometimes this includes just trimming off a skewed corner. Sometimes it means trimming an

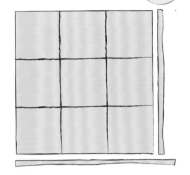

Squaring up

entire side to fit the others. Please remember that you don't want to trim off all of your seam allowance in trying to get your blocks to match, especially if you have a point that you don't want to "lose" during the piecing. But more on that later.

Piecing and Patchwork versus Quilting

These terms are often used interchangeably by most quilters, but they actually mean two completely different things. *Piecing* is the process of creating the top layer of the quilt, the part that requires you to cut it, sew it, and then to join all of the blocks and borders together to create what most people refer to as a quilt top. This is also often referred to as *patchwork*. In fact, in many European countries, the entire process of quilting is referred to as patchwork. Quilting, on the other hand, refers to the process of making a "quilt sandwich" of the three layers of a quilt and sewing through all three layers in order to create one finished, textured quilt. Quilting can be done by your own machine, by hand, or by an experienced "longarm quilter" who will take your quilt top, batting, and backing and do all of the quilting for you. Many prolific quilters choose the professional route whereas many who are starting out choose to do simple quilting on their patchwork at home as a way of learning the methods and of saving money. I highly recommend that everyone who has a love for the quilt world and wants to learn how the art works learn how to quilt her own quilt at some point. I started off quilting all of my own quilts on my home machine. I have since met and fallen in love with my local quilter, and I send every single one of my quilt tops to her. I am glad that I know how to quilt even if I choose not to spend my time doing it these days.

Pressing versus Ironing

Whereas we use both of these terms interchangeably as well, only pressing is actually helpful in the world of patchwork and quilting. Pressing means just what it sounds like. It involves lifting the iron up and then putting it down to press the seams that have been sewn. It does not include a lot of dragging and pulling and tugging at the fabric. Having said that, there is often the need to "make something work" in quilting just like there is in sewing. Sometimes your fabric pieces or blocks are not exactly like the others you would like them to be like, and you need to "iron" them into submission. Now, this isn't a good place to start, but I would be foolish to tell you that it won't be a necessary part of making your blocks fit and your quilt flat. So as a rule press; iron only when necessary!

In quilting, the direction of the pressing is also often very important. Most patterns mention which direction you should press the seam and how to press in alternate directions in order to get your seams to "interlock" when the blocks or rows are sewn together. Again, this is the ideal and is what we are striving for, but it is not the end of the world, nor will your quilt fall apart, if your seams are sometimes pressed in the wrong direction. The worst thing that happens is that you have a bit more bulk in some corners and all of your seams do not turn in the exact same way. Let's just say that worse things have happened!

Clipping Threads

As a notorious "non thread-clipper," I am going to advise you with a straight face to clip your threads as you sew. With so many different pieces and parts in quilting, the stray and hanging threads can easily multiply and become a tangled problem underneath your beautiful blocks. It is always better to learn those good habits up front. If you simply teach yourself to clip your threads as you work, you won't have to unteach yourself the bad habit of not clipping threads as you progress.

The Basic Tools We Need

The Big Three

To enter the world of patchwork and quilting you really need nothing more than what I like to refer to in my seminars as the "Big Three." As you progress through the craft and hopefully fall in love with it, you will undoubtedly acquire lots of other favorite tools and notions. However, I always like to dispel the myth up front that quilting requires too many expensive tools for someone to invest in. Other than a machine, there are really only the Big Three and, to be honest, they are not really that big or that expensive.

A Self-Healing Mat

Available at every quilt and fabric store, self-healing cutting mats come in a variety of sizes, colors, and styles. We all have our favorites and purchase different ones for different purposes, but I have found over the years that the 18" × 24" size is a perfect size for most people. It fits easily on most surfaces and accommodates most of the cuts that you need to do for basic quilting. One mat will last you through many a quilt and, most likely, many a year, although I do recommend replacing them when the grooves on certain lines become noticeable enough that you can see them when you stand above the mat. Those grooves will impede your ability to cut as accurately as you could without them, and they will actually dull your rotary blades.

A Rotary Cutter

Unless you are working entirely by hand and with scissors, a rotary cutter is an unbelievable time-, energy-, and frustration-saving invention for quilters. It gives you the ability to cut with the kind of precision that you need in order to make a quilt block. Either the 45mm or the 60mm size is a good choice, in my opinion. The size you choose depends more on the size of your hand and what you are more comfortable holding than anything else. For years I used the 45mm faithfully, but I have just recently switched almost entirely to the 60mm, and I love it. I think the 60mm cuts faster, and I actually love the larger size now, even though I loved the other size before. Either I am very fickle or my tastes have changed over the years. If you are unsure or have never worked with a rotary cutter before, I recommend you try out both in a class or from a friend before investing in your own.

The only other tip I have about rotary cutters is CHANGE YOUR BLADE OFTEN! If it looks like I am shouting at you, it's because I am. . . at both you and at me, actually. In my quest to save money in my earlier years as a quilter, I made it some kind of quest to change my blade as little as possible in order to save the money on the replacement blades. Now I think I just do it out of a lack of time to think about changing it, and I thank goodness that the folks I work with change my blades regularly whenever they get tired of the raggedy ones! Conventional quilting wisdom says to change the blade as soon as you can't get a good cut all the way across the fabric on the first try or when it leaves little threads after you cut. I would say that waiting until this point is probably already too late because you have gotten used to pushing harder and harder as you cut. My test lately has been to put in a new blade if I am unsure and see how much of a difference there is in the cut. I usually see a huge difference on the first cut, and I know that I have once again waited too long to change my blade!

A Quilting Ruler

Lastly you need a clear, acrylic ruler. There are many different sizes and lengths available, and as you begin to get a better understanding of what kind of quilts you gravitate toward, several of those sizes will become indispensable to you as you work. To start off with, I recommend the 4" x 14". It is my new favorite in that it is small enough to take with me anywhere and yet long enough to extend all the way across a piece of folded fabric when I cut strips for a quilt. I think it is the perfect ruler to start off with. Another good alternative is the 6" x 12". The 6" x 24" is the perfect size for longer cuts and border cutting.

Other Tools Worth Their Weight in Gold

Seam Ripper

Even though the joke around our studio is that we are not allowed to use a seam ripper because quilting is, after all a folk art, and no one but you will probably notice the error, a good seam ripper is a great tool to have. Look for one with a good feel and a handle that is easy for you to hold.

Design Wall

The visual perspective you get from seeing your blocks in front of you on a design wall is really quite invaluable. Even though this is a hard one for many people to manage due to space constraints, there are many creative ways to make yourself a design wall with the space you do have. All you need is a wide piece of white flannel and an available wall space. Outside of the standard hanging or standalone design walls, great examples that I have seen include closet sliding glass doors, pull-down roman shades, white flannel pinned to the front of a quilt that is already hanging in your house, and flannel pinned to closed, flattened curtains.

Tape Measure

A good tape measure needs to be soft and long, measuring at least 90". The short 60" ones are not that helpful because as soon as you sew a quilt that is larger than 60" you need to move the tape when you measure, which often leads to errors. The retractable tape measures are my favorites.

Thimble

I have tried to love those beautiful heirloom thimbles that get passed down from grandmother to granddaughter. Really—I have. Instead I use the inexpensive black leather thimbles with the little slit in the top for my fingernail. I know—I am definitely a cheap date in this category!

Bigger Tools Worth Investing In

Good Steam Iron

In this category I have not found that more expensive is better. The feature that you are really looking for is steam. You want good, strong, generous, problem-free steam to press those blocks into submission when you need to. My best advice is to ask your quilting friends or your local quilt shop to see what irons they have had the best luck with. You will find that everyone has had a good and a bad iron experience and they are just waiting to tell you all about it. You might be sorry you asked but you will get loads of information. Take notes!

Wide Ironing Board

I almost put this on my must-have list even though I know it's not really a deal-breaker. Ever since I have been quilting I have loved having an extra-wide 18" ironing board. They are available at several home stores and are becoming more popular. You do have to make your own ironing board covers when you burn through the one that comes with the board, but I think that is a small price to pay for that wide surface!

Cutting Table at the Correct Height

Most people cut at the dining room table, kitchen table, or a makeshift cutting table in their studios. I know this because I did it for years. If, however, you are going to be serious about your quilting, you are going to spend hours standing in front of your cutting space. Cutting at the correct height for your body can make the difference between happiness and serious shoulder and back pain. I am 5' 9" and my favorite cutting table is at 32". You are looking for a height that doesn't require you to bend down but where you can still get good pressure from your shoulder all the way across your cutting mat. Many quilt stores sell extension tubes that you can put on the bottom of any simple folding table to adjust it to fit your particular needs.

A Few of My Favorite Things

There are the things you need and the things that you love. I think you know what I am talking about here, right? Even though I am not much of a gadget girl, these are a few of my favorite things that either make my sewing and quilting life so much easier or that I have just grown to depend on over the years.

Bias Tape Makers

Bias tape maker

These little simple gems are easily one of my all-time favorite gadgets. You simply pull a strip of fabric through and it comes out as a ready piece of bias tape. It comes in a variety of sizes and is the only way to go for stems, basket handles, branches, and vines. Each package comes with simple directions.

Basting Glue

As a gal who never has enough time to finish all the projects floating around in my head, I am always looking for things that will make my job easier. One of the first years I was quilting and learning appliqué, I found these wonderful basting glue bottles that made pinning my appliqué pieces obsolete. With the little bottle, the skinny metal applicator tube and the wonderful "dry clear" glue, you cannot go wrong. Simply add little dots of the glue, which is easy to do with the thin metal tube on the applicator, to your appliqué piece and affix it to your background. Voilà, no pins, Mom! For more info on how to use this product, look at the "Appliqué" section on page 33.

Needle Threader

I am a little bit embarrassed to admit that when I hit the big 4-0, my eyes started needing help with the thread. Sad but true. So now I have a little needle threader gadget that sits on my studio table. Instead of struggling with the needle, it takes a quick minute to use the threader, and it works every single time. I don't leave home without it!

Good Pins

This is definitely one of those things that is a luxury and not a necessity, but I have fallen in love with a particular brand of Japanese pins, the "Little House" pins. They are super soft and go through my fabric like butter. To find your own favorite pins, try many different kinds from your friends. Every single one is really quite different in thickness, length, head, price, and feel.

Thread

Like many of the sewing notions out there, there can be a dizzying number of kinds and styles of threads in the notions section of any fabric store. Although I probably haven't tried most of them, I can tell you that I use neutral cotton threads exclusively. In recent years I have fallen in love with the Aurifil™ brand of thread due to its strength, feel, thinness, and lack of fuzz left in my machine. I pretty much buy it by the boxful and use it for all of my piecing needs, both quilting and sewing. In terms of other thread uses, my quilter exclusively uses soft cream cotton to do my quilting, and I use neutral YLI silk threads for my hand and machine appliqué.

Needles

You can choose from a large array of hand sewing needles on the market and each length and thickness is designed with specific characteristics in order to accomplish a certain task. As your sewing adventure continues you will likely find new uses for many of the needles out there. In this book, I talk about "Straw" needles for appliqué and "Betweens" needles for hand quilting. I choose Straw needles for their flexibility, thinness, and length while I am doing hand appliqué. I am completely attached to my favorite Straw needles! When it comes to hand quilting a quilt, on the other hand, Betweens needles are best for an entirely different set of reasons. When hand quilting you want a short, sturdy needle that can easily be pushed through multiple layers of your quilt sandwich. When choosing your first Betweens needle, I recommend buying a small variety pack to see which size feels best in your hand instead of assuming that the smallest will always be the best.

Your Machine

I am sure that there are entire chapters written about how to choose and make a decision about purchasing a sewing machine. I don't have that kind of expertise, but here is my two cents' worth.

I have had the same wonderful machine for the last ten years, and as long as I service her once every year, she never lets me down. I sew on a Bernina 1230. Yes, she's one of those machines from before they became more computerized. She never breaks; she never complains; and she never has any issues of any kind.

For quilting I recommend the following features as "must-haves" on any machine that you might want to invest in:

- A straight stitch, a zigzag, and a good buttonhole or overlock stitch for doing machine appliqué.
- A ¼" foot.
- A "needle down" option on your needle position.
- The ability to disengage your feed dogs comes in very handy as does a free-motion or "open" foot for free-motion quilting.
- A mirror image option for your stitches. I use this regularly when I am using my overlock stitch for machine appliqué and need it to go the opposite direction from the standard way it comes on the machine. I have thanked my stars for that option over the years!
- An attachment table is almost a must if you are going to do any kind of quilting. Without it, quilting is a struggle because your quilt doesn't have anywhere to fall and its own weight will be constantly pulling the quilt down and making quilting near to impossible. You can purchase an attachment table for most machines, but be sure you purchase the correct one as the shape of each machine, and thus the attachment table shape, is different. They are definitely not interchangeable.
- A walking foot is nice if you are planning on doing a straight quilt stitching line "in the ditch," crosshatching, or channel stitching. A walking foot also comes in quite handy for binding or when sewing many layers together because it avoids the pulling and shifting of the multiple layers during sewing.

For sewing I recommend the following features as "must-haves":

- A straight stitch, a zigzag, an overlock stitch for finishing seams, an actual buttonhole stitch for when you venture into buttonholes.
- A "needle down" option is wonderful for sewing as well because it enables you to easily stop and pivot your seam.
- A reverse button that is easily accessible is very handy for all those times you need to backstitch at the beginning and end of a seam.

Patchwork Basics

As I start to write this section I find myself wishing that you all knew me personally. Primarily this is because I wish you could see the slight smirk on my face and perhaps a little rolling of the eyes as I write all of these somewhat dry, basic steps and instructions. If you knew me, you would know that I am much more of a hands-on, "learn through your own mistakes and needs as you go" kind of girl. It's certainly the way I did it, especially with quilting, so I feel a bit phony telling you the many things you need to know before you can start! As I think of your process, I hope that you at least look through these sections, use them often as reference, and be on your merry way to learn to sew with your own style. Just don't ever say that I didn't tell you all you needed to know upfront!

How to Choose and Prepare Fabric

Chain Stores

Most of us, whether brand new to this craft or seasoned veterans of either quilting or sewing, probably received our introduction to fabric at a chain store. The rows and rows of delicious colors and

textures was something that drew us in before we even knew that sewing was going to be a passion in our lives. These stores usually have the best selection of sewing-related items, and they are a great place to start your sewing adventure. They carry cottons and felts and voiles and wools and every other kind of fabric imaginable. If your imagination can think of it, a well-stocked chain fabric store probably has all the fabrics and sewing notions that you need to make it. In fact, their large selection of notions is one of the main reasons I still go there today. Also their wonderful coupons can be used for some bigger ticket items! But there is more out there than just the chain store.

Local Independents

It is the local fabric shop that carries all of those delicious designer collections that we hear about in our favorite blogs and browse in our favorite online fabric shops or see in all of the wonderful quilting magazines out there. Your local fabric shop is where you can feel and touch that fabric. For most of us, that experience is indispensable.

It is also the local independent fabric store that, in my opinion, is at the heart of our quilting and sewing story. It is my local fabric shop where

Determining the Level of a Project

Just as in any craft or handwork, the spectrum of difficulty in both quilting and sewing is vast. Although this is not a comprehensive list, some of the pointers that I like to give my students include the following:

Quilting

- The bigger the block, the more simple the pieces both to cut out and to piece.
- Choose blocks that don't have a hundred pieces because the more pieces there are in a block, the more chances there are for discrepancies and also because it will take you that much more time to complete it.
- Avoid bias during the cutting process if you can. Many techniques these days (such as the one I show on page 23) use triangles that are actually sewn from squares, thus avoiding the dreaded bias stretch.
- Wait to do curved piecing until a bit further in your quilting journey.
- Choose lap or twin size quilts to start off with rather than a king size project of a lifetime. For your first projects, you really want something that you will finish before you get frustrated.
- Appliqué large pieces with little to no inner points and sharp curves when you are first learning. Most people get turned off to appliqué because they attempt something too complicated too early in their journeys.

Sewing

- Choose a project that has just a few pieces to start off. Because I am often introducing quilters to garment sewing, our girl's dresses often have only three or four pieces. That is a great place to start.
- Avoid patterns with a million little embellishments and finishing details. When you are starting out, those will just frustrate you and keep you from wanting to finish the project.
- Work with fabric that you know and understand. If all you have ever worked with is cottons, don't try knits for your first sewing projects.
- Try to look past the lingo on a sewing pattern to see if the basic construction makes sense to you. Go ahead and look up a few terms if you have to, but if the entire pattern uses a vocabulary that you don't understand, save that pattern for another time.

I began to take classes as well as taught those very same classes, and it is there that I started to consider fabric design. The sense of community, camaraderie, and learning that exists in any good quilt shop is worth its weight in gold. If you want to find others like you and share your sewing and quilting journey with them, it is the local fabric shop that is your best bet in finding others in your community that share those same interests. It is the local fabric shop that is usually able to answer your latest question, help you with your latest mistake, or point you in the direction of the latest book on the subject. You will most likely find some of your closest friends at that shop as well—because, after all, who else but a fellow sewer will understand your love of all things fabric!

Online Stores

Although I do believe that the local quilt shop is at the heart of our industry, a prompt and well-stocked online shop is also an invaluable resource, and it's good to know who your favorites are. No matter how hard they try, your local quilt shop just can't stock everything, and many local shops specialize in one style and don't carry other looks that you might be after. A good online store has what you are looking for, especially when you are looking for the latest designer print that you just have to have. Look for websites that are well organized and updated frequently, and ones that carry a wide selection of the style that you are looking for.

Designer Fabrics

Most of the projects in this book are made with 100% quilting-weight cottons that have been designed specifically for the independent fabric stores. Most are my Fig Tree designs, but I have also used a variety of other MODA fabrics and fabrics from other designer friends in our industry. Of course, as a designer myself I am just a little bit biased, but I think that the quality and the "hand," the vibrancy, and the wide array of design of designer fabrics are worth the slightly higher price tag that independents have to charge in order to stay in business. Wherever you decide that you want to shop given your budget or the fabric that you are looking for, I encourage you to support your independent fabric store in whatever way you can. I think they are still at the core of our industry and key to the community that thrives around both sewing and quilting.

Preparing Fabric

Given that these projects are made with designer cottons, not much prep work is required. Not only is cotton already the easiest fabric to work with, but for quilting I don't recommend washing your fabrics before cutting. Generally fabric comes off the bolt with one fold down the middle and in quilting this fold is used as the first step of fabric preparation for cutting, so I don't even want you to press it out. Literally, fabric off the bolt is how most of us use it for quilting!

> **NOTE:** If your fabric is of a quality that you are not sure of or it is a color or style that you are particularly worried about, such as a batik or a deep red or black, then I recommend testing a little piece to see if it will bleed. The easiest way to do this is to simply cut a square of the fabric, place it in a small cup of water and place it in the microwave until the water is boiling hot. Check to see if the fabric has bled at all. Take the fabric out, place it on a white paper towel, and dab. If it does not bleed with those two tests, which most good quilting cottons will not, you are good to use it as is.

Quick Cutting and Piecing Methods

There are so many different techniques and methods in the quilting world that I couldn't even begin to describe them all to you here and still have room left for the projects! But given that I tend toward simple, graphic designs that utilize the fabric as the star of the show, there are several basic techniques that I think are at the core of quilt construction. As your skills progress, I challenge you to branch out and try techniques such as curved piecing, using templates, or paper piecing. For me, even though I have tried those methods, my favorite way to work on patchwork quilting always seems to come back to the basics, those building blocks from which everything else comes. I admit that I do love to make the basics look more complicated than they really are, and I love that "a-ha" moment that my students have when they see the trick that I have used to make something complex out of basic squares and rectangles. But I do not believe that things in quilting actually have to be complicated to look that way. In that lies the trick of clever design.

Rotary Cutting

All of the quilt projects here use what we refer to as rotary cutting techniques as opposed to scissors and hand piecing. First you cut strips of fabrics from your yardage and then cross cut the strip to make squares and rectangles as called for in your project instructions. If your quilt uses triangles, you will most likely use the special triangle technique described later in this chapter or you will cut triangles from the squares that you have already cut.

1. Start by straightening up the left edge of your fabric. To do this, place the fabric on the mat in front of you and fold the fabric in half lengthwise—most likely this step will already be done for you as quilting-weight cotton comes off the bolt already folded in half. Fold it again, aligning the selvedge edges at the top and the folded edge closest to you. The left edge of the fabric will be uneven and you need to trim it up in order to have a straight line to start your strip cutting.

2. Lay your quilting ruler along that left edge of fabric. To make sure that your fabric is straight across, line up another ruler right next to it to determine that your fabric is laying at a 90° angle and that the strips you cut will actually be straight. This is officially the best way to determine that your strips will be straight, but I have to admit that after years of quilting I never do that anymore. Instead I just make sure that the fold of fabric nearest to me is lined up exactly on a horizontal line on my mat and that the selvedge edges on top are also more or less even and straight.

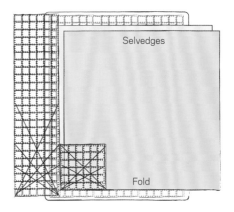

Step 2

3. With your left hand on the long ruler, fingers spread, and the pressure coming straight from the top and not an angle, which will cause the ruler to slip, use your rotary cutter to cut along the right edge of your ruler. Throw away your fabric scrap and your edge is ready for cutting.

4. Measuring over from your straight left edge, cut the strips the width in your pattern instructions. For example, if you need a 3" strip of fabric, place the 3" vertical line of your ruler on your straight edge of fabric and cut along the right edge of the ruler.

5. To cut squares and rectangles from your strips, place the strip in front of you horizontally opened up so that you have the original fabric fold on your right and the selvedges together on the left. Trim away the selvedge edges of the strip and square up the left side of the strip just like you did with the yardage. Begin to cut the required sizes and number of pieces as shown, starting from that straightened left side. Your strip will still be folded in half so you will be cutting two pieces at a time.

> **NOTE:** If you are left handed, the process will be the same except that everything will be straightened up and cut from the right side instead of the left.

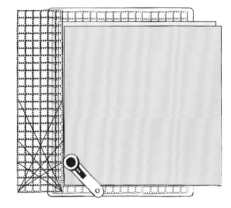

Step 3

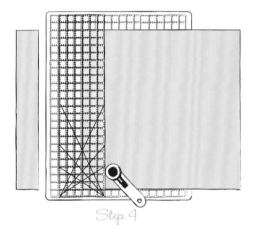

Step 4

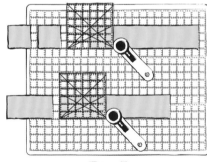

Step 5

Rotary Strip Cutting

When cutting the pieces you need for the blocks of a quilt, I recommend that you don't just cut the pieces for one block at a time. Instead, cut all of the same pieces at the same time, if possible from the same strip. Often our tendency is to want to cut each block one at a time to see the quilt grow block by block, but this method adds hours of work to your process. Instead, doing the same step over and over and then moving on makes the process so much more efficient. When you are making 36 of the same block, efficiency becomes key!

HINT: Even if the directions are not laid out that way, it is often easy enough to take a look at the instructions for a particular pattern and choose to cut all roofs at the same time or all the window pieces from all the various fabrics in the quilt.

The directions in this book are usually laid out with rotary cutting in mind, and this is what I recommend for most quilt projects unless it is particularly or uniquely useful to cut your blocks one at a time. Most often this is because I think it will be easier to cut all the pieces from one piece of fabric before you move on to your next fabric. This is also done as a huge time saver.

This principle holds true whether or not the pieces are from 1 piece of fabric or 20 different fabrics. If you do the same action over and over again, your pieces will be more accurate, your process will be *much* faster, and you will reach your goal quicker.

One of my favorite things to do is to dedicate an afternoon or, depending on the size of the project, a day to cutting. I turn on my favorite music or a little marathon of my favorite television show and I get to cutting. Somehow it ends up feeling less tedious to me to cut everything at once and just be done with that step altogether.

Strip Piecing

I do love the process of sewing and don't want to come across as someone who is all about the end result and the speed with which it takes to get there. However, there are several techniques in quilting that make the most out of your time and have the best end result. This is one of them. Many different kinds of blocks and block sections yield themselves to

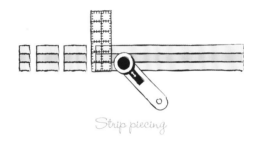

Strip piecing

strip piecing, including any kind of simple square patchwork or checkerboard blocks, 9-patches, rail fence blocks, and others. In strip piecing you sew full length strips together in the necessary fabric combinations first, press them as indicated by the pattern, and then cut them into the desired sections and pieces instead of cutting each small piece separately and then piecing afterward. It is a wonderful way to work through one of the more tedious portions of your process.

Chain Piecing

There is nothing exciting about some of the steps in the process of creating a quilt, but they just have to be done. Cutting out the original fabric is fun, strip piecing has quick results, pressing and revealing the blocks at the end is possibly every quilter's favorite part, but sewing the little pieces together one after another is, in my opinion, one of those things that you just need to do in order to get to where you want to be! To make that

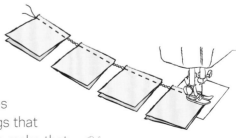

Chain piecing

process faster and more accurate, use chain piecing, which is nothing more than feeding the same section of your block through the machine, continuously, one after another, without stopping or cutting threads in between. Sometimes I chain piece 50 sections at a time. I then stop at the end, pull out the entire chain of 50 sections, snip the threads in between each one and move to the pressing portion of the job. You have to love your chain gang!

Pinning

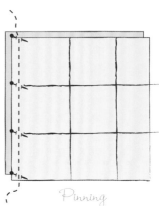

Pinning

Because I am someone who looks for ways to not pin whenever it is at all possible, I advise you to do as I say and not as I do on this one. One of the key things you are looking for when you are quilting is to have certain corners and points match one another. The best way to get that to happen, especially when you are first starting out, is to pin in those places so that your fabric can't move. In fact, if your pieces don't match up exactly to begin with, pinning them exactly where you want them to go helps you make them do what you want, and your pieces match because you pinned well. The best places to pin are on each end of your block and in any place where seams are supposed to match with one another. Always pin vertically into the block and not horizontally within the block. Horizontal pinning tends to shift.

Triangle Units

Another one of my favorite quick-piece methods is used when you sew a fabric square to a rectangle or larger square on the diagonal in order to create a triangular piece on a background piece. This method is probably the main building block of a majority of the quilt blocks that I work with. It is a method worth getting to know.

> **HINT:** Traditionally this was done (and is sometimes still done by many quilters) by cutting out two triangles and sewing them together. All I can say to all the bias in those pieces is "Oh, my goodness!" As a general rule I always opt for any method that uses squares and rectangles to create other shapes because it avoids the time-consuming and error-producing reality of using pieces with bias. Maybe this comes from my years of being a quilt teacher, but nothing is more frustrating for a new quilter than to find that they cut everything correctly only to have everything stretch and not fit during the sewing process due to bias.

This method creates accurate triangles without the use of bias. I do realize that this method is not always the most economical in terms of fabric because you cut out the back of the squares, but I have found that it is definitely the most accurate method for the least amount of extra work, and it yields wonderful results every time, which is always worth a couple of extra inches of fabric.

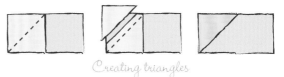

Creating triangles

1. Press the square of fabric that is going to be sewn to the background in half on the diagonal, RSO.
2. Place the square of fabric on top the background fabric that is usually a rectangle or larger square (RST) and sew that square to the background piece on the pressed diagonal.
3. After you have diagonally stitched the top square to the bottom background fabric, open the sewn triangle and fold back the fabric until its corner matches the corner of the bottom piece. Press out.
4. Trim only the leftover back piece of the top square that you sewed. The reason for this is that if you have any inaccuracy or something in your piecing shifts, the dimensions of the complete bottom piece retain an accurate size for your section. It helps create more accuracy as you piece that section into your block.

> **HINT:** I want to mention that a lot of quilters who are used to cutting off all that excess fabric ask me about the potential problem of bulk in those sections, and my answer is always the same: This method is all about getting more accurate pieces for block constructions, and I have personally seldom encountered enough bulk due to that extra piece to be a problem for piecing or later for quilting. Having said that, feel free to cut out your background fabric if you are feeling especially confident in your piecing!

Adding Borders

I don't know why, but it still always surprises me when people have different quilt phobias and dislikes than I do. As if we were all the same person! But adding borders is one I shared with many quilters for many years, and it is still not my favorite part of the process.

I think that usually when I am done with the blocks being assembled and I can see the quilt together, I feel done and don't want to spend the time and energy it takes to add the borders. This is especially true if there is more than one border to the pattern. All that is to say. . . I am with you on this one!

I want you to know that as quilt designers, we know that many people strongly dislike some part of the process of border creation or assembly. Some people hate choosing them. Some people hate measuring them. Some people hate all the pinning and easing involved if the sides are not all equal. Whatever your particular border phobia happens to be, hopefully I can talk you through enough of it so that you can get those borders on and move on to the end goal of quilting and binding!

Breaking My Own Rule

The other disclaimer that I want to mention with this method that I love so much and recommend is that if the square on top is much lighter than the background piece, cream for instance, this method does not necessarily work. If you cut out the back of the square but leave the darker background intact, the dark fabric shows through after it is pieced and quilted. In this instance you have the choice of either cutting out both and dealing with the potential accuracy problems or leaving in all three layers and dealing with potential bulk problems. I have tried and had success-ful results with both depending on the size of the block and the triangle at hand.

At the Frame Store

I know we all have those favorite prints sitting around the house somewhere, unframed, perhaps rolled up, and just waiting for the time or energy to take a trip to the frame store. That is what all those unfinished quilt tops remind me of. They are just sitting there, ready for a frame of their own.

I like to think of borders as frames for my quilt, or, if I have several borders, a couple of mats and a frame like the kind you would have added to your favorite print or painting at a professional framing store. Sometimes you want that matting to be mellow and understated, simply there to bring out what is already in the painting. Other times you want that mat to be a vibrant part of the overall design, something that really brings the whole design together, accenting the feel or the flavor of the entire piece. Whichever type of border or border grouping you are going for, the fol-lowing are my tips for successful borders:

1. I never choose a border until my quilt center is finished and I can hold it up or pin it on a design wall and take a good, long, hard look at what it needs. The center of each quilt really dictates what fabric and what width of borders it needs. Many options will be just fine, so do not worry about ruining your quilt with the wrong choice. Often, the perfect choice becomes evident the second that you hold it up next to your quilt.

   Of course, the minute I make a rule, I always want to break it and have indeed broken this first one several times in my quilting career. There have been times when my border fabric has been the entire inspiration for the quilt design itself. In that case, of course, the border came first and everything else was worked to go with that fabric. It has felt a bit like working backward in those instances, but it has been a good mental exercise for me.

2. The size of the border should be tied to the design elements of the inside of your quilt. There are many different opinions on this, but in my experience, unless you have one single outer border, the width of the first border shouldn't be any wider than either a dominant portion of the quilt block or the sashing in the center of the quilt. This is especially true if you are

working on multiple borders because your eye often wants to see a smaller inner border that helps to close up and set off your pieced center.

> **HINT:** I refer to this term of trying out border fabrics as "auditioning" borders. Pin your quilt or even just a folded portion of your quilt on a design wall, or, if you need to, lay it out on the floor. Audition as many different fabrics as you can find until one "sings" to you and also think about the widths that correspond to the widths of dominant pieces in your blocks. Most likely one of those widths will be the right width frame for your quilt top and you will usually know it the moment you see it. This auditioning process is also a perfect thing to do in a class or with sewing friends because different pairs of eyes see completely different things during the auditions.

Thrice Then Once

I know that there are many "deep sighs" when it comes to measuring and deciding on how to cut the borders for your quilt. And I recognize that shortcuts are very tempting here. However, I confess that from personal experience in my earlier quilting years, I have found that measuring your borders instead of merely laying down your strips, sewing, and cutting off what is leftover, no matter how tempting, is not worth the outcome. And even though I am not one to be strict with rules and quilting "musts," I will be the first one to tell you that well-measured borders can often be the key to a fabulous final outcome! In order to have a successful, flat quilt without wavy borders or a bulging middle, you really need to measure your borders.

1. When you are measuring your quilt for your borders, there is a quilting saying out there that goes something like this, "measure thrice, cut once." Now I know that thrice is not a word that most of us ever use, but you get the idea! In my experience, it is a very good idea to measure each measurement *three times* to ensure that you have the correct amount. This means that you lay your quilt on a flat surface and repeat each measurement three times—or more if your numbers are coming out different each time. In this instance it is really better to be safe than sorry. Cutting a border too short because of a bad measuring job is one of the most frustrating mistakes you can make for two reasons: You are so close to the end and also there is so much fabric waste involved. Often you don't have enough fabric to fix your mistake!

2. Measure your quilt top through the vertical middle and cut two of your borders to that length. Usually in order to have the needed length, you need to have pieced that length from two strips. If you don't want to have to piece your strips to get the needed length for your border, then be prepared to buy a lot more fabric and to simply cut the border lengths along the length of the fabric for a continuous piece.

3. Repeat Step 2 for the other two sides after you have sewn the first two borders onto the quilt.

At the Border

Unless you are a perfectly accurate piecer (kudos to those of you out there who qualify for that title), your borders and your quilt will be slightly different sizes, and you need to start the process of easing in the fabric. This is a practice that we use a lot in quilting, and whether you have to ease in a lot or a little bit of fabric, the process is worth the outcome of an even quilt. When pinning the borders to your quilt, I recommend that you press your border in half to find the middle point and that you do the same with your quilt top. Match those two middle points and pin them together. Also pin the borders on at the two ends. Ease the border in or out as necessary in between those pins, taking care to distribute the fabric evenly across the whole quilt top to avoid ripples or tucks. Sew and press out toward the border.

Finishing Techniques

Even though these might not be the glamorous parts of the quilting process, the choices we make on the finishing of our project can often be some of the most important for the final outcome. Choices such as batting might not be seen on the outside of your project but can truly accentuate or hide the look and feel that you are going for. In addition, choices such as quilting and binding are, in my opinion, some of the most important in the entire process as they can bring your patchwork top to life and finish it off with the perfect ending. In your excitement to finish your project, I hope that you don't overlook these last couple of steps.

Batting

There are a few things that I think of that can really add a lot of flavor and extra character to your quilt. Batting is one of those things. There are what seems like a hundred different varieties of battings out there these days, but they can be broken down into two main categories: natural fiber batting—which is usually cotton, but more recently can be bamboo or soy—and polyester. The main difference between the two kinds of batting is that one is natural and one is not. Also one variety is primarily flat or "low loft," (cotton) and is the other is primarily fluffy or "high loft" (polyester). Within those categories there are many variations, blends, and other options. When I look at batting I am looking primarily for the drape that it will give my quilt and the cotton content that it has in order to create that vintage, "crinkly" look that I am often going for with my quilts. So I use cotton or bamboo battings exclusively, and am looking for the lightest weight batting with the nicest drape possible. My favorites include Mountain Mist Cream or White Rose, Quilters Dream Request, Fairfield Soft Touch, and Elan Luna Blend. Now, I need to remind you that I live in California and don't experience much of a winter of any kind. If that is not your reality, then by all means still stick with cotton but go for the heaviest cotton possible, which is usually Warm & Natural by Mountain Mist.

NOTE: Because I never prewash my quilt fabrics or my batting, when the quilt is washed it has a chance to shrink a little and "pucker" just a tiny bit, giving it that well-loved feel that so many of us cherish about our quilts. It is one of those instant gratification things that I love to do and I often come back impatiently to the dryer to see if the new quilt is ready to come out and be used!

Layering and Quilting

If you have read all the way through to here and have worked through the process, you are nearing the finish line. At this point you can decide that you are done and hand off your quilt top to your trusted longarm professional and move on to your next project! However if you would like to try your hand at quilting your project on your home machine, follow along.

You need to make what we refer to as a "quilt sandwich" as described below. You should cut the batting and backing 2" or 3" larger than the quilt top on all sides so that you don't have to struggle with getting the quilt top to match the back exactly. For several of the quilts in this book, it is necessary to sew two lengths of fabric together to make a backing the size you need. Always piece the backing horizontally unless it is necessary to do it otherwise due to the size of the quilt. Trim away the selvedges before sewing the lengths together and press the center seam allowance open.

1. Place the backing, wrong side up, on a flat surface. Smooth out any wrinkles and secure it to the surface with masking tape on the four corners. I like to use blue painting tape and stick the quilt to my wood floor. If you have a low loft carpet, it is a bit tougher to get a good flat shape, but it's doable. In that case, pin the edges into your carpet. It is not really possible with a high loft carpet. Your backing should be taut but not stretched.

2. Spread and center the batting over the backing and smooth any folds or wrinkles.

3. Center the pressed quilt top over the batting and smooth the quilt out from the center toward the edges. The quilt top edges should be parallel to the edges of the backing and you should have anywhere from 2" to 3" of batting and backing showing around the edges of the quilt top.

4. For machine quilting, I like to use small rustproof safety pins to pin the layers together. Begin pinning in the center, working toward the outside edges and placing pins every 4" to 5" or so. For hand quilting, baste the layers together using a sharp Betweens needle in size 10 or 11 and thread that you can easily see on your fabric. Baste diagonally from corner to corner first, and then continue stitching at 4" to 5" intervals.

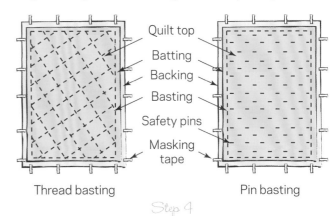

Quilt top
Batting
Backing
Basting
Safety pins
Masking tape

Thread basting   Pin basting

Step 4

5. Hand or machine quilt the layers together. If you're machine quilting, remove the pins as you go. Remove the basting thread when you're finished hand quilting.

6. Trim the backing and the batting even with the edges of the quilt.

> **QUILTING TIP:** For those of you attempting quilting on your home machine for the first time, you basically have two options: straight stitching, such as in the ditch or cross-hatching, or free-motion quilting. If you are opting for straight stitching, attach a walking foot to your machine and either stitch in the seam lines of your project (which is known as *in the ditch*) or mark your project with chalk or tape and stitch diagonal lines in both directions at your desired intervals (which is known as *cross-hatching*). If you are going for the more relaxed free-motion quilting then get ready to move those hands! I highly recommend that you draw yourself a sheet of the "puzzle" diagram, put an old needle on your machine, disengage your feed dogs, attach a free motion foot and practice your "puzzle" lines on the paper. Practice as many times as you like until you think you have a feel for how to move your hands around the quilt. When you think you are ready, remove the paper, change out your needle and try it out on a scrap "sandwich." After that, you are ready to free motion. Just remember what I tell every single one of my classes: The first couple of times you do this, you will make mistakes, you will stitch over your lines, you will make points where you wanted to make curves, and your shoulders will really hurt when you are done. But it will get easier and you will be really proud of the result!

A Bit More about Quilting

I know I have already given you several tips and opinions on this topic throughout this basics section but I just wanted to reiterate the fact that quilting can really make or break a project. Beautiful heirloom quilting, custom fit to the size and feel of your blocks, can turn any good but ordinary quilt top into an amazing work of art. I cannot tell you how many times I have handed over a quilt top that I was satisfied with, but not in love with, to my quilter only to get it back to be awestruck by the beauty of it all. Quilting adds a huge amount of texture, feel, and personality to your quilt, so just make sure that you choose your quilter and the pattern carefully.

If you have a more modern-feeling quilt, continue that look by choosing a modern type of quilting design, such as something simple and geometric. Channel, in the ditch, clamshell, diamonds, and large cross-hatch all come immediately to mind for me. Many styles of meandering or whimsical stitching also lend themselves to more modern or whimsical quilts.

If you have spent weeks of your life on an elaborate traditional pieced quilt top, go the extra distance, or, in this case the extra dollar, and ask for quilting that matches. Beautiful wreaths, feathers, custom block designs, and cross-hatch all lend a classic, traditional feel.

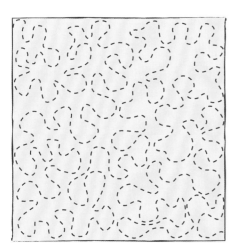
Puzzle diagram for free-motion quilting

Lastly, if you have created an appliqué masterpiece, be sure that the quilting doesn't overwhelm or overtake the work that you put into the appliqué. Appliqué quilts are often best served by outline stitches, meandering or stippling in the backgrounds, or soft repeating patterns such as small cross-hatching, small clamshells, or small echo or channel lines. If you have very large appliqué pieces, it is usually a good idea to do simple outline or decorative stitching even in the center of the design in order to tack it down to the batting and prevent the appliqué shape from "poofing" up or cupping due to the lack of stitching in it.

Binding

Binding is one of those great hand projects that can be done pretty much anywhere. I have bound entire quilts in front of the television, in the car, while watching soccer practice, and on the plane on the way to a trade show! After you've sewn down the batting on one side by machine, the rest is handwork. I use exclusively straight binding for my quilts, as do most of today's quilters. The only exception to that would be if you have curved edges on your quilt. See the "Bias Binding" section for more information on that.

Straight Binding

I like my binding to be on the thinner side, but I still want to have enough to nicely cover my binding and to not have to struggle to get it to cover the stitch line on the reverse side. To this end I cut my binding strips 2¼" and make double-fold binding. I like to trim my quilt sandwich a tiny bit wider than the ¼" needed in order to help "fill up" the binding as it rounds over the outer edge. I then turn all the remaining binding as far as it will go to the back of the quilt.

1. Join 2¼" strips as shown in the diagram. Place the fabric right sides together at right angles to each other. Sew across the diagonal from the top-left corner to the bottom-right corner. Trim the excess fabric and press your seams open. Keep adding all the strips together in this way until you have sewn together all the strips called for in your quilt pattern.

2. Press the 2¼" width of fabric in half RSO all the way down the length of the joined strips. This will most likely be a very long piece, so just keep pressing. Press all the joining seams open.

3. Begin stitching the binding to the top side of the quilt through all of the layers using a ¼" seam allowance, leaving a tail of about 9" of binding and starting somewhere in the middle of a side.

4. Stop stitching exactly ¼" from the corner of the quilt, backstitch, and cut threads.

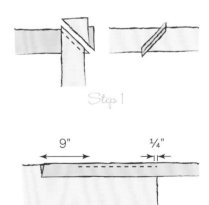

Step 1

9"   ¼"

Quilt top

Steps 3 and 4

5. Turn the quilt to the next side. Turn the strip up so it makes a 45° angle and then fold it back down on itself. You are basically mitering the corner with this step.

6. Begin stitching from the edge, again using a ¼" seam allowance. Continue down that side until you get to the next corner. Repeat the corner procedure described in Step 5.

7. When you get approximately 9" away from where you started stitching, backstitch and cut the thread.

8. At this point, you have two loose ends. Overlap the fabric ends and mark where they overlap by exactly 2¼". Trim the excess fabric at that mark. Place these ends at right angles to each other, RST, pin in place, and sew from the top-left corner diagonally to the bottom-right corner. I always hold my finger right on the bottom-right corner to help ensure that I sew a straight line right toward it. You want to end up right at that corner. Open up your binding to make sure you sewed it correctly. It should fit exactly over the unsewn opening. Trim the remaining fabric to a ¼" seam and finger press the seam open.

Step 5

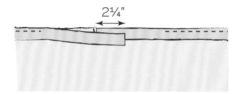

2¼"

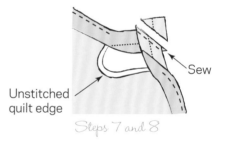

Sew

Unstitched
quilt edge

Steps 7 and 8

HINT: I have discovered that if I merely overlap the fabrics to measure how much I will need to trim off, I almost inevitably cut a tiny bit more than I need and then struggle to not tuck the fabric when I am sewing it down. Now when I overlap the fabric edges to determine where I will trim the excess, I pull them fairly tight along the quilt. This seems to work like a charm every time and gives me the perfect length for finishing off my binding.

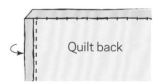

Quilt back

9. Sew the remainder of binding to quilt.

10. Turn the binding to the back of the quilt and stitch by hand using a whipstitch.

Step 10

Bias Binding

I use bias binding when I have scalloped or curved corners on my quilts or when I really want to see the pattern on the fabric shown on the 45° diagonal when sewn to the quilt. Gingham, for example, looks great as binding when cut on the bias. It isn't nearly as complicated as some people believe it to be. What follows is the simplest way I know of to make regular bias binding.

1. The strips are cut to the same 2¼" width as straight binding and joined in the same way as described earlier. There are two things that are different: You need to calculate the total amount of inches around your quilt and alter the way you cut the initial strips.

2. Calculate the amount you need by measuring one side and the top of your quilt. Multiply each of those numbers by 2 and add them together. This is the perimeter of your quilt. Add 18" to that total and you have the total length that you will need of binding strips.

3. Start with at least ½ yard of fabric so that the strips you cut are longer, preferably ⅝ or ¾ yard. Fold your fabric up into a large triangle (at this point it will be too long to cut with a 24" ruler). Then fold it down again. You should now have two folds on top of each other.

4. Barely trim off the fold of your right triangle so that you now have four cut edges that are all lined up together. I like to do it this way because I can then cut two strips at a time. Even if you are a tiny bit off the bias, it doesn't matter so don't stress too much about it.

5. Begin cutting your strips from this first cut, all the way across the fabric, 2¼" each time. Remember that you are cutting two folded strips at a time.

6. Keep track of how many inches each cut of two pieces yields toward the total that you need. Keep cutting until you have the necessary length in inches.

7. Join just like you would straight binding.

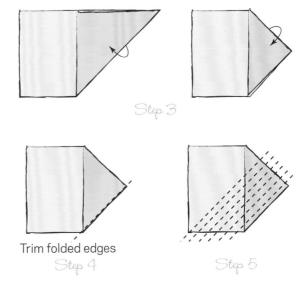

Step 3

Trim folded edges
Step 4

Step 5

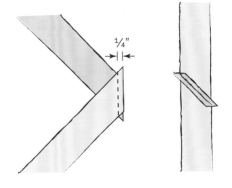

1/4"

Press seam allowances open

Step 7

A Few Special Quilting Techniques

There are so many other things that I would love to share with you. Over the years of quilting, I have come to love and rely on many different techniques, tips, and methods as a way of making my quilting life more enjoyable. For me it is both the process of the work and a good and pleasing result that make for a helpful technique in my opinion. Here are a few of my personal favorites.

Appliqué: The Starch Method of Applique

In quilting, appliqué is the term used when you are sewing one shape on top of another, background shape. Usually this piece is an organic shape that cannot be pieced geometrically and so it is added on top of the quilt instead of pieced into it. Appliqué is seen as an entire category and style of quilting and stands on its own as a quilting art. For me appliqué was something I endured for the sake of my design until I discovered the appliqué method described here. Although I tried many different methods before this one, none freed me or gave me the confidence and, yes, the desire to work with any kind of appliqué shape in my designs. Since discovering and working to perfect this method, I have grown to love appliqué for the creative design element it is in my design process. I have found that it wasn't so hard or so scary after all.

Supplies

- Can of spray starch
- Small craft brush
- Freezer paper
- Thin permanent marker
- Paper scissors
- Stiletto

- Small iron
- Your regular appliqué supplies, which for me includes Straw #10 or #11 needles, YLI thread in neutral tones, Roxanne™ Glue-Baste-It

NOTE: If you find that you like appliquéing as much as I do then there are many special tools and materials out on the market that will help you tremendously with the process, including freezer paper that has already been doubled, specialty stilettos, tiny craft irons, and more.

1. Trace your appliqué shape to the shiny side of a piece of freezer paper. Press that piece of freezer paper onto a second piece of freezer paper so that you are working with a double piece—dull side to shiny side so that what you are left with is a double piece with one side shiny and one side dull. The double thickness helps prevent your templates from curling. Your marked line is now enclosed inside the freezer paper template.

2. Cut the shapes out on the line.

3. Iron the freezer paper templates to the wrong side of the fabric. Cut a scant ¼" seam allowance around the fabric shape. Clip into the curves and around the points. Remember that sharp curves need more clips and soft curves need fewer. For inner points, cut a few threads shy of the template.

4. Leave the paper in place and paint starch onto the backside of the fabric seam allowance with a small paintbrush. (Spray some starch into a small jar or into the cap so that it has time to "defoam" before you paint it on.)

5. Press the seam allowance back onto the freezer paper shape, taking care around corners and curves. A stiletto is very helpful in pulling the points all the way in as you are ironing down your seam allowance and in assisting you with the movement of the fabric as you press. In the absence of a stiletto you can use the tip of sharp scissors or a skewer.

6. If you have excess fabric on an outer point, trim it down after you have starched down one side of the point. If you ever press more than you need, simply reapply starch to the portion that you need to re-press.

7. When working with an inner point, use the tip of your iron to press down one side and sweep the fabric in and over to the next side. Work with inner points as little as possible, but if necessary I take the tip of my iron and press directly into the point to secure the point and any stray threads. This always does the trick of getting clean inner points.

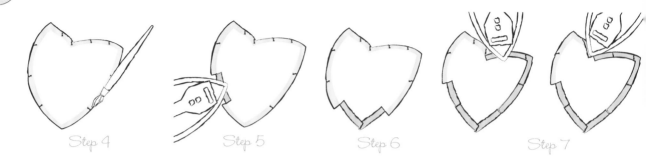

Step 4   Step 5   Step 6   Step 7

> **HINT:** Those small hand irons work really great, but I've used my regular iron in a pinch as well. If you are going to be using a large iron, just look for one that has a good point on the end. That will be the part that you are using for this method.

8. When the ¼" seams are all ironed down, pull out the freezer paper along a straight away and what you have left is a perfect shape. You can reuse that same paper shape many times before it falls apart.

9. Glue your appliqué shape down onto your background using pin dots of basting glue on the back of the starched-down seam allowance. When you're done you have a perfectly turned appliqué image ready for whatever kind of finishing you like, whether it be hand stitching or finishing by machine.

> **HINT:** When cutting my appliqué background for a project, I always cut about 1" extra all the way around. Often while appliquéing the background frays or distorts due to the pulling in of the stitches. By cutting your background piece larger, you have a bit of extra to work with and you can trim it up when you are done.

A Standard Appliqué Stitch

1. I use YLI #100 weight silk thread exclusively for three reasons. I can use minimal neutral colors on all of my fabrics because the thin thread blends effortlessly with all the colors in its color family. Also, the thread literally disappears into my fabrics every time even if my stitch is a little less than perfect! The thread comes in a whole array of colors but the ones I use are cream, light beige, medium caramel, black, red, and olive green.

2. When your shapes are starched and glued down to your background fabric, hold the piece you are working on between your thumb and index finger, bring your needle up through the background fabric (the knot will be on the back side of your fabric), then through one or two threads of the turned edge of your appliqué shape.

3. Insert your needle straight back down into the background fabric only insert it straight across from where your needle came up. This way the portion of the stitch that shows on the front side is so minimal that it is close to invisible.

4. For your next stitch, come up about ⅛" away from the last stitch through the background again and again pick up only one or two threads of the turned edge of your appliqué shape.

5. Continue in this way. Finish your thread on the back of your work with a knot.

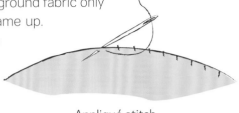

Appliqué stitch

Inside point   Outside point

> **HINT:** Take two stitches right at an outer point or inner point to strengthen those areas and to ensure that any loose threads there are tightly sewn in.

Working with Wool

Personally, when it comes to appliqué, I love to mix fabric with wool as often as I can. There is something unique about the pairing of cotton and wool that gives your projects a certain charm. My attraction for using wool is twofold. First, I love working with wool because of the texture and depth that it creates in a quilt or any type of project. There is nothing else like the interplay of cotton and wool to bring out the colors and the shapes of the appliqué. Second, and not any less important, is that wool does not have to be turned under and stays raw edged when appliquéing because it does not fray. This makes it a wonderful medium to use for small, intricate pieces that you might not want to tackle if you were using only cotton fabric.

Here are several tips for working with wool:

1. You can clip any stray wool threads after you cut the shape or after you appliqué if necessary.

2. The best stitch to use is a small, even whipstitch, but some people prefer to use a small blanket stitch (both have a similar effect visually) taking care to go in far enough to catch a sufficient portion of the wool.

3. Using YLI silk thread in a neutral tone works great; the thread completely disappears into the wool. This is what I do in all my wool appliqué. An alternative is using a single strand of DMC floss or another thicker thread for stitching that is more noticeable and decorative.

4. A small machine buttonhole also works quite nicely, making the process even more simple for those of you who aren't avid hand appliquérs.

5. Take care around outside points, stitching more closely together and "defining the point" with your stitches.

6. Overlap a couple of stitches at the end for strength.

Playing with Precuts

During the last couple of years fabric manufacturers have started producing precuts of their latest designer collections as a way to market the lines and give people an opportunity to see the entire collection. Precuts are little stacks, bundles, or rolls of various widths that come with a variety of fun names such as Charm Packs, Layer Cakes™, and Jelly Rolls ™, and they give the quilter an opportunity to use a little bit of every piece of fabric in a certain collection without having to buy large quantities of yardage of each of those fabrics. Precuts are a great way to make a simple quilt; you don't have to worry about the process of choosing a color palette as well as having some or all of the cutting already done for you. Sometimes having all that accurate cutting already done the moment you sit down to sew is just the push that you need to whip up a wonderful project that you can complete and enjoy a few short days later!

Precuts are also great jumping-off points where you not only get to see and play with all of the prints in a favorite fabric collection, but you can also add other fabrics from your stash or favorites from that line to make your own unique combinations. Over the years I have designed many patterns that lend themselves specifically to precuts to give my customers an option to work

with these fun little packages and still create quilts that feel unique and personal. As I will discuss more in Chapter 4, precuts are a perfect way to create a base for a scrappy-feeling quilt. So if you come across one of these yummy little bundles at your favorite local fabric store, you might just want to pick one up to see how it might spark your creativity.

Embroidery as Embellishment

Even though I don't usually embroider and most of my projects don't have that type of handwork in them, there has been an amazing resurgence of embroidery and different varieties of handwork in the last couple of years. Our generation has definitely rediscovered the age-old craft, and embroidery is being added to everything from small handcrafted projects to giant pieced quilts and seemingly everything in between. I mention it here solely to spark your curiosity and to remind you that if you enjoy handwork and embellishment, there are plenty of projects in this book that lend themselves to it. A little simple embroidery in the centers of the Buttercup pincushions would be so charming, as would some simple white or cream embellishment on the Little Bloomers pillow or the Maison version of the Blossom quilt.

Chapter 3

Basics of Sewing

Several of the terms that I used and discussed in Chapter 2 could just as easily have fallen under this category and vice versa, so take the placement of the terms themselves with a grain of salt. If you remember from my personal story, I progressed from quilting into sewing, and so I always start with the quilting side of things as I work through my sewing process. I am also completely self-taught in the sewing department. By "self-taught" I mean that I have learned from books and the lovely ladies who sew for my company on a daily basis, but I have never taken an official sewing class or gone to school to learn sewing. So it is possible, or likely, that some of the things I do are different, or perhaps even backward, to the ways others might teach you. But my methods work for me, and so I would like to share them with you! In the same vein I want to note that this sewing section if far from all-encompassing and is not meant to be a complete sewing dictionary. Instead I am focusing on only the things that you need to be familiar with in order to work on the fairly basic projects that are presented in this book.

The Basic Terms We Use

Regardless of what new adventure we are about to undertake, there always seems to be a new set of vocabulary that we need to familiarize ourselves with. In our house recently I have been learning the sometimes odd vocabulary of a teenager (learning a foreign language has sometimes seemed easier than this)! In sewing, as well, there are words and phrases that most sewers take for granted but that feel like Greek to many of us who are just starting out. For now, don't worry about remembering what all of it means, but do read through it all. Each time you need to know what it means, come look it up and pretty soon you'll be speaking "sew" without even knowing it. I'm not sure though if I will be as lucky with speaking "teenager"!

RSO, RST, and the Rest of the Alphabet

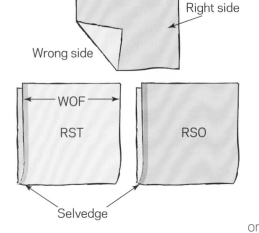

There are some quick sewing terms that are used all the time in patterns. *RSO* means *right sides out* and refers to which direction the fabrics are being sewn or placed together. The right side of the fabric is the good side—the side you want to see when you are done! *RST*, or *right sides together*, is the opposite of RSO. *WOF* means *width of fabric* and is something I refer to when I want to make sure that you are cutting or using an entire strip or piece of fabric all the way from selvedge to selvedge.

Straight, Cross, and Bias

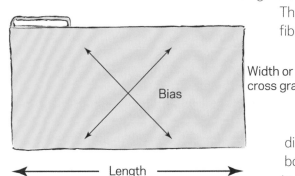

Something that we all need to be aware of when cutting and sewing is that fabric behaves differently depending on the direction in which it is pulled. It has the least amount of stretch or "give" on the length of grain where the fibers are the strongest. This is the length of fabric as it is rolled on the bolt. These fibers are also referred to as the *warp*. The cross-grain direction, otherwise known as the *weft*, has a bit more give to it, but the give is not much more than what you get on the length, and it is usually the direction that you cut quilt pieces and garments to give your fabric a tiny bit of give. The 45° angle in either direction is where the fabric behaves quite differently both for good and for evil, as we like to joke. It is referred to as the *bias* and it provides quite a bit of stretch, which you can easily see by pulling any piece of fabric in this direction. In quilting, bias is something we like to avoid at all costs because it moves and stretches and makes piecing with precision quite difficult. In sewing, you can utilize the bias for wonderful results in things such as circle skirts, flounces, and other ways of making fabric move and shape in lovely ways. When cutting straight-forward patterns, however, or if it is not stated as something that you should be doing, stay away from cutting your fabric on the bias and stick with the straight of grain.

Seam Allowance

Perhaps one of the biggest differences in quilting and sewing is the importance and size of the seam allowance. As outlined in Chapter 2, the ¼" seam allowance is queen in the quilting realm. In sewing, on the other hand, an accurate seam allowance is neither nearly as important nor as criti-cal as long as you are consistent. I have found this a hard adjustment to make as I have branched out more and more into sewing. Not only that, but the traditional sewing seam allowance is ⅝". I have tried to find out why it is so large from sewer friends of mine, and I am still stumped. Many sewers today use a ½" seam allowance when sewing, and for the purposes of this book I used a ½" seam allowance for the sewing projects. (Really I usually ended up sewing more of a generous ⅜" allowance because I am constantly fighting the urge to go back to my beloved ¼" quilting seams!)

The Basic Tools We Need

There are a few basic tools of the trade that I have grown to embrace and find that I turn to as often as I do my long-time quilting tool companions. Many of these tools can be and are incorpo-rated into the quilted projects in this book, but they definitely come from the sewing side of things. I know that many of you who are coming from the quilting side will find some of these products or tools foreign, but I encourage you to give them a try. They are truly wonderful and make your sewing life so much easier.

Tape Measure

Whereas we use hard acrylic rulers of various lengths and sizes in quilting, it is the tape measure that is the sewer's best friend. When I talk about a tape measure for sewing, I am referring to a soft, ribbon-like tape measure and not the hard metal one used by building contractors. Person-ally, my favorites have always been the small, retractable 120" tape measures, but the old-fashioned ribbon tapes that you might picture your grandma using are just as effective for most sewing tasks.

Tracing and Freezer Paper

A roll of tracing paper and a double-long roll of freezer paper are two products that my studio is never without. I know that most sewers come from a long tradition of using tracing paper and prefer it to any other kind of pattern paper. Given that I have come from quilting, I brought my love of freezer paper into my sewing adventures with me. Let me tell you why.

Freezer paper is available at any grocery store along with all of the other kitchen papers, such as tin foil and plastic wrap. It is sturdier than tracing paper and, more importantly, it can be pressed to the fabric. So when you have traced a pattern onto freezer paper, instead of using pins, you simply press it to the fabric, cut it out, and peel the paper off. It is fast, very accurate, lasts forever, and does not tear. Most importantly, it does not require a single pin—which is undoubtedly what I love most about it! I do realize that it probably won't work for larger garment pieces primarily because most of us don't have a pressing surface that's sufficiently large, but it is the loveliest product for anything else. Freezer paper is also what I use for all of my appliqué templates. I do use tracing paper for a variety of other uses, including quilting pattern tracing, working on initial garment mock-ups (because the tracing paper is more malleable), and instances where I have to trace lots of small details, such as an embroidery design (because tracing paper is much lighter and easier to see through).

Interfacing

Interfacing comes in a variety of strengths, types, and fabrications, and the number of choices at the store can be overwhelming. The two main types of interfacings are sew-in and fusible. Both are readily available in woven, knitted, and non-woven versions. They come in a variety of weights, ranging from heavy to sheer weight. I stick primarily to non-woven, medium-weight, fusible interfacing that can be easily attached to the fabric. In my projects, I usually use interfacing to strengthen the area around a piece of attached hardware, such as a purse magnet, or to strengthen or give more structure to an entire piece of fabric.

Fusible Fleece

When this type of fabric is referred to in the projects, it is not the kind of fleece you might be thinking of that creates a cozy blanket. Fusible fleece is nothing more than a thicker, sturdier version of interfacing. It is a lofty fabric that resembles the look of quilting batting but has an adhesive layer on one side that adheres to other fabric when the two are pressed together with an iron. I use it as a way to give structure and body to otherwise soft or light-weight fabrics such as cotton. In this book, I have used fusible fleece on many sewing versions of a dual project.

Thread

Again there are hundreds of choices in the world of thread, with as many applications and uses as there are kinds. Both for utility and decoration, threads span the gamut from cotton to silk to polyester, and they come in every thickness and color imaginable. The thread section of any fabric store can be a bit overwhelming to a new sewer.

Because I don't work with many specialty fabrics or unusual decorative stitching in my own sewing, I primarily use three kinds of thread—neutral piecing or sewing thread, silk thread for appliqué, and coordinating accent thread for topstitching. For all of my sewing and piecework I use a 100% neutral cotton thread in a 50 weight (which is fairly standard). I look for a thread that doesn't leave much lint in the machine because it seems that some days I go through a spool a day! For appliqué work, whether by hand or by machine, I use neutral 100% silk threads from a single manufacturer, the YLI brand of threads. Lastly, when finishing the details on many sewing projects, I switch to a cotton thread that matches whatever color fabric I am using. Often the thread in the machine works just fine, but when the color is much darker or different in tone I change it to something that yields a better result for finishing work.

Needles

There is a lot to learn about how needles are sized, named, and categorized. For the projects in this book, I recommend a Universal 80/12 sewing needle for your machine. I also recommend that you replace it more often than I do! Conventional wisdom tells us to replace a machine needle after 10 or so hours of sewing use or, of course, when it is visibly bent, broken, or damaged in any other way. As you get familiar with your own machine, you will be able to hear when something is not quite right as the needle starts making more of a clicking or popping sound as it is going through the fabric. For hand work, especially appliqué of any kind, I recommend a Straw needle, size 10 or 11.

Scissors

I use three scissors in my sewing adventures: a pair of 8" Gingher dressmaker shears, a pair of small but sharp embroidery scissors, and a pair of basic bent spring-loaded craft scissors. I use the dressmaker's shears for cutting out patterns; the embroidery scissors for clipping threads and cutting out appliqué and other small shapes; and the spring-loaded scissors for almost all my general fabric cutting. Most importantly, I must add, is that your fabric scissors have to be saved for fabric use exclusively. No lending it to the kids for paper and craft projects! Any other cutting dulls your good scissors very quickly, and you should keep them separate from other scissors. This is definitely one of those tips that I didn't listen to until I saw the effects myself!

Muslin

Almost every project in this book was a prototype before it was a reality. In many instances it was five prototypes before I made a final choice on size, shape, and combination! Given that for any more-involved project, especially a garment, you might want to make an inexpensive prototype before you cut into your lovely designer cottons, muslin comes in quite handy. If you do a lot of sewing, you might even want to invest in a bolt of muslin. It is neutral in color, and it is cotton, so it moves the same way your finished product will. Usually it's the least expensive fabric in the fabric store.

Just a Few More Favorites

These are the sewing helpers that you can certainly start sewing without, but they make your sewing process so much easier, faster, or more enjoyable that you should consider having them on hand. I have acquired all of these items over time and don't regret owning any of them.

Hemostats

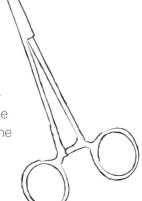

Possibly my latest favorite tool, the hemostat is a clamp-type instrument made primarily for the medical industry but used by all sorts of crafters for various uses that require manipulating in a small or narrow space. I have found that using hemostats is better than any other method for turning tubes, straps, and handles RSO. You simply insert the hemostat into the tube, push the fabric onto the tool until you can grab the inside end, clamp the hemostat in place, and slowly pull the entire tube out in one move. This tool has seriously saved me hours of my life. I recommend getting the longest hemostats you can find. My favorite size is 10".

Water Soluble Pens

I have to admit that water soluble pens make me a tiny bit nervous because I don't know exactly how they work chemically, but I have found that they are a life saver in many instances. In the past I would have used chalk for most of my marking needs, but I don't always like the ease with which it rubs out and that it won't show up well on many of my lighter or busier fabrics. As my alternative, I have turned to the water soluble pens that mark in a brighter color, such as blue or purple, and disappear completely when sprayed with a bit of water.

Light Box

The light box does feel like something of a luxury because for years I simply used a backlit window and some good old-fashioned elbow grease to trace whatever I needed. These days I use a simple light box to trace patterns onto fabric or other mediums that you can't see through with the naked eye, such as tracing or freezer paper. Mostly the light box saves me from looking silly to the neighbors as they walk by and try to figure out what I am doing!

Working with Hardware

There are many different kinds of hardware in sewing, but the types that I use in this book are primarily for bags and purses. Believe it or not, hardware in general is something that scares many quilters into not wanting to make a project at all! I guess it is the same as the fear of sewing ¼" seams that fit perfectly together for those of you who are coming from the sewing side of things. I admit that for years I avoided anything that had a zipper, a grommet, a snap or anything resembling a button! Nowadays, I seem to add them to anything I can because I love the professional-looking details that these simple embellishments give to the finished look of my work.

Grommets

Grommets are simple ways to add a little finishing touch to your bag or other project. Grommets come in sets with male and female parts as well as the small tool that you need to place on top of the grommet in order to attach it to your project. The process of adding them requires nothing more than a hammer, a towel, and a hard concrete surface. Each package has quick, straightforward instructions.

Magnets

Magnets could not be simpler to add as a finishing detail on the flap or inside of a bag. They usually consist of a female and a male side along with two small washers, and they come in a variety of sizes and finishes. They're very easy to use. For added fabric strength, I recommend adding interfacing to any spot where you plan to add a magnet. From personal experience I have learned that you should affix the magnet before you finish off or bind your piece!

D-rings

A D-ring is one of the most commonly used pieces of hardware to attach a strap or handle to the body of a bag. It is usually made from metal and is shaped like the letter D. Often it is used in conjunction with swivel or snap hooks to finish off the professional finished look that nice hardware can give a project.

More Hardware to Think About

Although I did not use any of these other pieces of hardware in the projects for this book, I do recommend that you familiarize yourself with both of the following items as they are worth learning about, and they are not as difficult to use as you might first think.

1. Try making a simple buttonhole in a scrap of fabric. Almost all machines these days have a buttonhole function that makes this process very simple. Personally I recommend trying to make a buttonhole when you have time to play around and not when you are stressed out because you actually need to add one to a garment.
2. Add a zipper to anything! I had a serious zipper phobia until the seamstress who works with me showed me the easiest method for adding zippers that I had ever seen. You don't even need a zipper foot. Look online for zipper tutorials or check out basic sewing books for more information on attaching zippers. Several of the Fig Tree & Co. standalone pattern packs also contain good zipper information.

The Difference between a Quilter and a Sewer

You will see the technical and vocabulary differences between quilting and sewing pointed out and sprinkled throughout the various sections of the basics chapters, but there are a few underlying principles I thought it important to add. I realize this is somewhat intuitive, but on a basic level, quilters are trained to sew things together precisely so that the pieces lay flat. They think and design in graphic terms and in two dimensions. Sewers, on the other hand, are by definition three-dimensional thinkers as they visualize size, shape, and proportion. They are not necessarily that married to precision and exactness because there is a lot more ease and flexibility in sewing than there is in quilting.

By craft, quilters learn to sew very straight, cut very precisely and watch small details such as the points of a triangle shape to make sure they are pieced into the seams at exactly the right point so that it is not lost. That third dimension—not to mention the addition of finishing details such as hardware and special stitching—is something that many quilters think they cannot tackle. Having trained their minds on making small exact pieces fit together, many quilters think that they have lost the ability to think outside of that particular box.

Sewers, on the other hand, think much more about proportion—for example, the curve of a seam and how it will look on the shoulder or where the straps of the handbag will hit the curve of the hip. They think about how a fabric might look after it has been pleated or how to finish a seam so that it will look nice on the outside of a garment. Their details are completely different than that of a quilter, and their minds think more in terms of finishing touches and wearability. Sewers concentrate a bit more on the big picture—the movement and the feel of a piece. Sewing hundreds of little pieces together to create a design does not immediately make sense to many sewers and might even seem like a waste of time. After all, in that same span of time, one could make a skirt and wear it!

Even as I write this, I am struck again by how much we can teach one another and how much our common bonds of love of fabric, color, and texture are the basis around which we can rally together. There is such a lovely marriage that is already starting to happen as designers cross over from one world into the other and are inspired by what they encounter. As the two worlds come together more and more, the creations that the meetings of these two minds will bring will be fantastic to watch!

The Basic Principles of Sewing

Stating that you should understand the fabric that you are working with might seem obvious, but it's something that we often overlook in our excitement to start on the actual project. Who wants to think about the mundane when there are beautiful fabrics to play with! I assure you that taking a few minutes to familiarize yourself with the materials that you are working with goes a long way to ensuring the success of your final project.

Preparing Fabric

Working with fabric that will be worn, played with, or regularly handled requires a different sort of preparation than what we are used to when preparing quilting fabrics. Even though most of the sewing projects in this book use the exact same 100% designer cotton fabrics that are used with the quilted projects, the preparation can be a bit different. First off I recommend that you wash any cotton fabric you are going to use for something that you will want to wash later, such as the apron, bags, placemats, or other home projects. In my opinion, it is also important to wash them in the same manner you plan on washing the finished product to maintain the same effect to the fabric. The extra step of prewashing these fabrics ensures that your finished project holds up and does not shrink or distort for years to come.

If the objects themselves are quilted, you can choose to wash the fabric after it has been quilted if you like the slightly puckered, vintage look that the fabric has after washing. If you prefer a straighter, flatter appearance then wash the fabrics before you quilt them.

Fabric Width

Most of the cotton fabrics that I work with come in the standard 44"/45" width off the bolt. As mentioned previously, they are folded in half on the bolt, so the folded piece is often approximately 22" wide. The other two popular widths are 54" and 60", which is the width of several of the linens I use.

The unfinished side end, where you can often find the designer name and collection information, is called the selvedge. Subtracting the selvedge edges and the rows of tiny holes where the fabric was attached to the rollers as it was printed and manufactured usually yields a useable width of 2" or 3" less than the stated width. In the patterns, I usually assume 42" width of useable fabric on standard cotton bolts. The length of the fabric refers to the length on the bolt itself and is the yardage that you are purchasing.

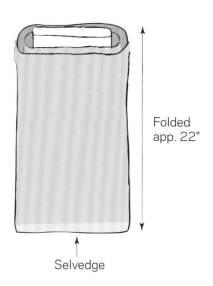

Folded
app. 22"

Selvedge

If you are working with a novelty or directional fabric, such as an involved border stripe, the design is almost always printed in the direction of the length so that you can determine how much of the stripe you need instead of having the design be dictated by the width of the fabric itself.

Cotton

As I have already mentioned, most of the projects in this book are made with 100% designer cottons. Cotton is a fairly simple fabric to work with because it does not have much stretch; it

Sewing Hint

Here are a few tips for success when working with laminated cotton:

1. Don't wash it as it is fully wipeable and cleanable and is not meant to be a washed fabric.
2. Always keep it rolled while not in use as creases are often hard to remove after they're set.
3. Try to minimize using pins during your sewing process as they leave small holes that do not heal after the pins are removed. In the book projects I try to keep the pinning to within the seam allowance or in places where I know another piece of fabric will be later added on top. Clothespins and binder clips make good substitutes for straight pins.
4. Before you start working with laminated cottons, you need to know that it doesn't play as nicely as standard cotton and won't cooperate if you try to feed the laminated side through your machine. There are several different ways that you can avoid that problem, such as:
   - Sew pieces right side together whenever possible to help avoid the friction that happens when you try to sew on the laminated side.
   - Add binding to your seams as you sew two layers together to provide your presser foot something other than the laminate to work with.
   - Place a piece of tissue or tracing paper on top of the laminated piece of fabric that you are working on. I have found that the piece underneath goes slowly through the machine, but the piece on top needs the tissue paper in order to not snag on the presser foot. When you are finished with that seam or topstitch, remove the fabric from your machine and slowly tear away the tissue paper on one side of the seam. The perforations of the needle should then make it simple to remove the remaining side with ease.
5. Press the fabric on a lower setting through a pressing cloth and watch for any changes in your laminate. If you have never pressed the particular laminate you are working with, experiment first on a scrap.

does not move; it is usually colorfast; it is most often a plain, non-textured weave; it is soft; and it comes in a wonderful array of beautiful prints. As you become more confident in your sewing and want to branch more into garments, many other fabrics such as blends, knits, and silks are wonderful alternatives to work with.

Laminated Cotton

Laminated cotton is another type of substrate that I have used in several of the projects in the book, and it requires a whole different kind of handling. Laminated cotton is exactly what it sounds like—a standard 100% cotton that has had one side laminated in order to make it waterproof and wipeable. Unlike oilcloth or vinyl, which are completely different kinds of products, laminated cotton is simply a covered cotton fabric that can be used in any way that cotton can.

Linen

Linen is a slightly thicker, stronger natural fiber than cotton. It wears a bit longer and is more absorbent than cotton, but it wrinkles worse than its cotton cousin. These days it comes in an array of beautiful colors that lend a wonderful feel and texture to many projects. I have used natural-colored linen, which comes in a gray/taupe kind of color, in several of my projects. I love the feel that linen adds to projects. Read more about linen and the effect it can have on projects in Chapter 4.

Working with Patterns

I have already covered this to some degree under other topics, but I just wanted to mention a few other things about patterns. I am a huge proponent of tracing your patterns and keeping the originals intact. I have had too many experiences and heard too many sad customer stories of lost, ripped, or misplaced patterns. Keep the originals with the book or pattern and take the few minutes to trace the pattern onto freezer or tracing paper so that you will always have a back up. I don't think you'll be sorry.

Also remember that although quilt patterns can't be "altered" because the whole point is to get them to fit exactly together, sewing patterns carry a lot more forgiveness with them. If you like the bag pattern but would prefer it to be a tiny bit bigger, smaller, rounder, or wider, feel free to add or subtract a little from the pattern to make it your own. Just remember that if there are multiple pieces, take care to see if any of the other pieces are affected by your alterations.

Lastly, none of the patterns in the book have notches or other traditional sewing markings on them. This is primarily due to the fact that I just don't sew this way. When pieces have to be lined up, I point out how to find the middle or where to start pinning or how to ease in or out to get the desired result. It is also due to the fact that most of these projects are smaller in nature and notches and other sewing markings are not that necessary. I have also found that notches scare people! I know that sounds funny, but those of you who are not used to reading traditional sewing patterns probably understand what I am talking about. I have found that the fewer traditional terms and sewing techniques I use, the more accessible the patterns are to quilters and many brand-new sewers.

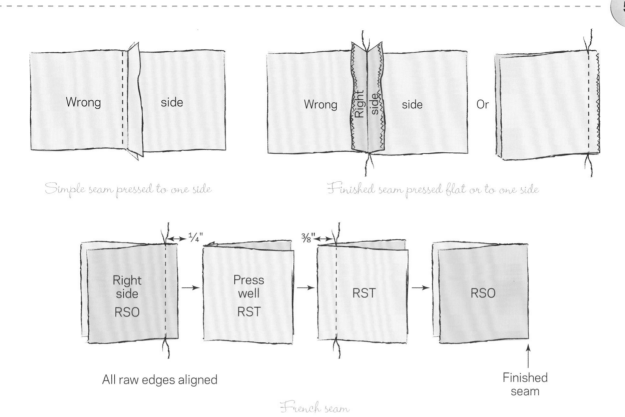

Simple seam pressed to one side

Finished seam pressed flat or to one side

French seam

Finishing Seams

Quilting basically uses a standard flat seam that is pressed in one direction or, in some cases, pressed flat. You do not really have to address any other types of seam or seam finishing. In the sewing projects I have used a few other techniques. I have used the flat seam, but I wanted to finish the raw edges to create a more clean finish. The most simple way to finish the raw edges of a flat seam are by zigzagging them in such a way that the right side of the zigzag basically falls right of the fabric, thus enclosing the raw edge in something that resembles a serged edge. I have used this in several of the laminated cotton projects as well as some of the more simple bags that didn't need a lining.

I have also shown you how to use a French seam in the Boardwalk Beach Tote. A French seam is basically a fully enclosed seam on both sides and gives you wonderful results with a very clean, professional look. You create it by first sewing the wrong sides of your fabrics together. I know it seems wrong but it isn't! It is a perfect seam for the inside of a bag or tote that doesn't have a lining.

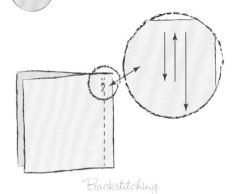

Backstitching

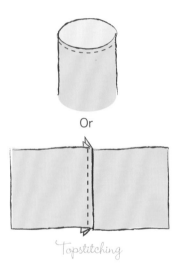

Or

Topstitching

Backstitching and Topstitching

Backstitching refers to the process of starting to sew your seam and then stitching backward for ½" or so in order to secure your seam. It is good to get into the habit of backstitching both at the beginning and at the end of your seam. *Topstitching*, also sometimes referred to as *edge stitching*, is sewing a stitch line on top of an already-sewn seam as a way of adding structure, definition, or decoration. Sometimes a topstitch is exactly what the seam needs in order to stay in place, such as on the top of a purse where the lining is trying to peek out from behind. Other times, a bit of topstitching with a complementary thread adds a wonderful finishing touch to your project.

Linings

Linings add a completely finished and polished look to the inside of a bag, a tote, or many a garment. Especially in bag making, the lining is often almost another bag that is simply slipped inside the outer bag to create a finished inside. For those of you who are not fans of the extra time it takes to make a lining, remember that you can always finish off your seams in any number of the ways discussed and bypass the step of lining altogether. That said, I do think it is quite lovely to open up your bag and see a lovely interior made from one of your favorite fabrics peeking out at you!

Single-fold Binding

A bit different than the standard double-fold binding that is used for quilting, *single-fold binding* is something you want to use when you don't want all that bulk that double-fold binding gives. On the edge of a sleeve or on something that is meant to have light movement, such as the Dear Betty apron, a single-fold binding gives you the same nice finished edge without all the bulk. Single-fold binding has only one thickness of fabric that wraps around the edge and the seam allowances are folded inside the binding itself.

1. Fold your binding strip in half lengthwise, RSO, and press. Open your fabric strip and fold and press each long side into the center fold. This creates four even sections divided by three even folds.

2. Open your binding strip and line up a raw edge of your binding with the raw edges of your project, RST. Pin in place. Sew the binding to the project.

3. Turn the binding up and over the raw edge, enclosing them. Fold the binding back down on the inside of the project.

4. Making sure that the last fold is tucked under, whipstitch the binding to the inside. As an alternative, you can also machine stitch the binding on, but be sure to sew from the right side of your project. Sew just to the right of the existing binding seam, stitching slowly to make sure that you are catching the inside folded seam as you sew.

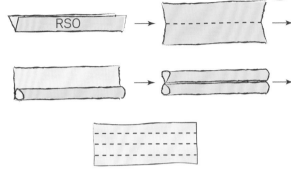

When opened: 3 folds/4 sections

Step 1

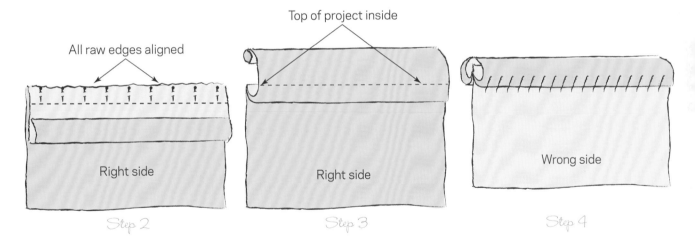

All raw edges aligned

Top of project inside

Right side

Step 2

Right side

Step 3

Wrong side

Step 4

To finish binding, whether single- or double-folded, on a round project such as a sleeve or top of a bag, add the following finish:

1. When sewing the binding to the project, leave a few inches free at the beginning and stop sewing when you reach 2" from where you began.

2. Extend the two free pieces so that they line up together and finger press both of them where they meet and touch the project you are sewing them to. Pin the strips together here. This is

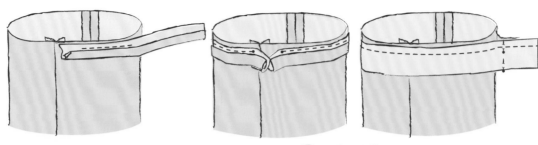

Steps 1 and 2

Step 3

where you want your joining seam to be. Pull the strips away from the project to avoid catching the project in the seam as you sew and sew the binding ends together along the two finger creases. Trim the ends.

3. Press the ends open, and finish up sewing the binding to your project. Finish as noted in the previous set of steps.

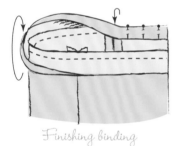

Finishing binding

Snips, Clips, and Wedges

Doesn't that sound a bit like vocabulary you would find at the hair stylist or perhaps a cheese counter? Instead these three simple little goodies make your curves lay flat and your corners not bulky. In all three cases, you want to make sure to snip only as much as you need, not coming too close to the seam. Contrary to popular belief, I have sometimes found that clipping is not necessary at all or that less is more! So I recommend experimenting with the amount that you need instead of assuming that more is always better.

Snips or clips are tiny little cuts that you want to make along the outside of a curve in order to help when you turn the fabric. The cuts separate into wedges on their own because that is what the fabric wants to do as it spreads around the outer curve. How far apart the snips need to be depends on the depth and size of the curve, but I start off with every ½" or so and then snip more if I need to.

Any time you have a corner, you should clip the corners at a 45° angle in order to prevent bulk. Clipping the excess seam in these instances helps you to get a corner that actually looks like, well, a corner, and not a big mess!

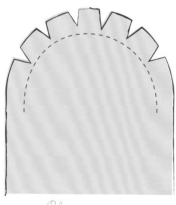

Clips in a curve

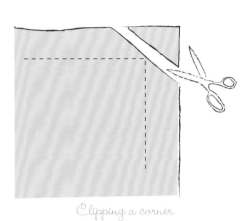

Clipping a corner

Wedges

Wedges or notches are angled snips where you cut a little of the fabric out—you guessed it—in a wedge in order to help the fabric turn better and lay flat. This is usually done on the inside of a curve to get rid of some of the excess fabric.

A Few More Useful Sewing Techniques

These last embellishments or finishing techniques are some of my favorite "tips of the trade," so to speak. Sometimes it is those small, thoughtful details or a quick technique tip that makes the difference between a ho-hum project and a stellar finish that you can be really proud of.

Pleats and Tucks

Pleats and tucks are different ways of adding body or visual interest to a garment or bag. Both of these decorative elements are wonderful ways to practice adding a bit of your own touch or personality to otherwise straightforward projects. Seen as functional sewing constructs by many, they are among my favorite ways to add a quick bit of style to many of my projects!

In the pleat family, I love the clean, traditional look of box pleats and inverted pleats. Box pleats are basically two folds of the same width turned away from one another to form a flat pleat in the center of the two folds.

Inverted pleats are pretty much the opposite: two folds turned toward one another that meet in the center and create that same pleat underneath the folds themselves, such as in the center of the My Audrey Purse. I have also used half of a pleat on either side of the center in the My Audrey Purse.

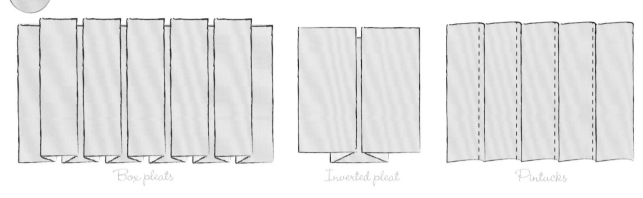

Box pleats   Inverted pleat   Pintucks

Tucks are traditionally folds of fabric that have been partially or completely stitched in place on the right side of the garment. In children's clothing in particular, pintucks or tiny little tucks are often used to add a decorative detail. Sometimes a little tuck here or there is all a project needs to make it a classic standout.

Ruffles and Gathers

Ruffles or gathers are another one of those romantic details that can add so much personality to an otherwise plain project. In fact, that is all that needs to be added in order to transform an ordinary pillow or little dress into something lovely. Full instructions for ruffling are given in the Little Bloomers project, but here are a few general pointers.

First, read the method in Little Bloomers, and trust me when I tell you that you really want to use a string. When you have, you will never want to go back to machine basting stitches. Let's just say that the string never breaks!

Second, ruffles can be single or double, which means that they can one sided or double sided (so that the right side of fabric is on both sides). I prefer the double-sided version both for its versatility and for its more substantial feel.

Also, as a general rule, you want to have anywhere from one-and-a-half to two-and-a-half times the width of your project for the ruffle. You know your style and can probably predict if you like a fuller or less full ruffle, but it is always better to err on the longer side and trim some off if you find that you have more fullness than you like.

Lastly, remember to distribute the fullness of the ruffle evenly over the entire project so that you don't have portions that are different from one another. At the same time, I usually recommend leaving the last ½" of a project flat to help it be sewn into the seam allowance.

Stuffing

My favorite stuffing to use in any pincushion or stuffed toy is 100% cotton stuffing. I love it for its feel and the wonderful results I get with it even though it is more expensive than the standard polyester stuffing available in most craft stores. When working on pincushions or small stuffed objects, I use a mix of the stuffing and crushed walnut hulls, which you can purchase as birdcage or lizard litter at your local pet shop.

NOTE: A good stuffing trick for pincushions or other small items is this: When you think that you have stuffed enough, keep stuffing!

When you have plenty of walnut hulls in your piece, use the cotton stuffing to round out the shape of the pincushion. I use my hemostats to grab a small piece of stuffing and place it exactly where I want it to go, which is yet another wonderful reason to have your own hemostats!

Standard stuffing is perfectly fine if you're making or amending pillow forms. However, in that situation I recommend buying already-prepared pillow forms unless you have a very specific pillow shape or size in mind. Foam is also another good pillow stuffer for seat cushions.

Remember that most stuffing and lumping problems are due to the fact that you have added too much stuffing at once into one spot, or you have stuffed pieces that were too big.

Chapter 4

Creating a
Color Story

Color is the absolute beginning of any project for me. Although many designers begin with the quilt pattern in mind or a particular bag design they would like to tackle, I start with a color palette that is creating a story in my imagination. Most often it is something that I cannot get out of my head until I start working with the fabric. With the color comes the design, the style, the function . . . the story. But it is the color that gets me creating in the first place.

Where Does Your Story Start?

Color seems to be one of those things that many people are either fascinated by or terrified of. You might think that in a visual field such as sewing and quilting that you would find more than your fair share of folks who are fearless with color and how to work with it and, of course, there are those people among us. More often than not, however, it is one of the main places where sewers of all ages and traditions get stuck. It seems that even in textile arenas, working effectively with color is a challenge to many.

One of the ways that teachers and lecturers like to get sewers to think about and understand color is to introduce and explain the principles of the color wheel. Now, don't get me wrong, I think that the color wheel is a wonderful tool in many ways. However, in my experience as a quilt teacher, brief teachings on the color wheel often prove to create quite the opposite effect. Many people leave a lecture about the color wheel more fearful of color and how all the rules apply to it than they were when they came in.

I believe that a much better place to start is at the beginning! I think that one of the most important things to learn in the world of color is to know what you really like, what inspires you and what you are consistently drawn to. This might sound like a simple idea, but the truth is that most people—even many crafters, sewers, and quilters—aren't sure of what style they like or what color combinations they prefer, and so they struggle to find pleasing palettes that yield the kinds

of results they are after. To figure out what you like, you need to start by looking around at what you seem to choose and gravitate toward in various areas of your life. I encourage you to look at what appeals to you not only in fabric styles, but in home decorating colors and dishware colors, giftwrap, stationery, clothing, and gift items. Open the doors to your closet or open your drawers and you will likely discover some themes that appeal to you. My friends chuckle at the dresses I wear in any given season as they are often in the exact same colors as the palettes I am working on in a current collection.

As you train yourself to look at your choices and preference, soon enough you will begin to see your own "trends." Don't be afraid of whatever color palettes you seem to be drawn to whether they be bright or muted. This will be your first step in choosing well for your quilt and sewing projects.

I realize that some might disagree with this perspective as there is always something to be learned in the process of creating any art form, but I am a firm believer that a finished quilt, bag, or pillow can be only as pleasing to you as the initial color palette choice. What I mean to communicate by this statement is not that there isn't any value in the hand sewing of the item or that the process of working with your hands is meaningless and that the result is all that matters. Instead what I mean is this: If you love the initial fabric selection, chances are you will love the finished product. If you feel mediocre about the fabrics before you ever start, no amount of technical finishing or quilting expertise will make you love it in the end. Of course there are moments when we are surprised or a particular palette grows on us and our tastes change, but in most instances that first fabric choice will largely dictate your final love of your finished project. Technical expertise is inspiring and amazing to look at, certainly, but if you think about what first draws you to a particular quilt or hand-sewn project, your answer will most likely be the color palette or how the colors and fabrics worked with one another. You will, of course, notice amazing workmanship after you get up close and personal with the item. The craftsmanship might even be the thing you remember and feel in awe about as you walk away. But it was not likely the first thing that drew your attention. There is something about color that affects us quite strongly, no matter who we are or whether or not we realize it. Color is a powerful tool that is used and studied by many. My experience in sewing is that it is the very most important place to start.

Color the Fig Tree Way

For our purposes here, I would like for you to throw out everything you have ever learned about the color wheel. Well, perhaps not everything, but please do not let yourself be bound by any rules that you know about color theory. Traditionally when we are taught about the color wheel, one of the basic tenets is that there are warm and cool colors. Instead, I like to say that every single color on the color wheel can be warm or cool depending on what has been used to make that color. That is, of course, also true of any fabric print with a variety of colors in one print. It can feel generally warm or cool depending on the various color elements and proportions within.

If you have not already figured this out, I love the warm side of each color and am drawn to it almost instinctively. Over the years I have learned to work with many different styles and palettes, but the ones I am drawn to again and again are the ones that I consider to be warm. As I begin to create a palette, whether it is for a fabric collection or for an individual project, I always start with a cream base. What I mean by this is that many fabrics have a white base, making them cooler in

appearance. Their basic undertone is white or gray. Some fabrics even have a purposeful cool base—a blue tone—to whatever color palette is on that fabric. I stay away from those fabrics. Fabrics with a cream base, on the other hand, have cream as their lightest tone and are warmer in general. Reds tend more toward tomato reds—orangey and soft. Greens turn more limey, Granny Smith apple, or chartreuse. Blues move all the way over to aqua and sea foam, both of which are blues with large amounts of yellow and slightly green overtones. Pinks are most likely to be peach and apricot. Even blacks and grays can be warm or cold with undertones of red, yellow, and brown versus blue. Most people would be amazed at the huge difference they would see if they laid all the solid black fabrics in their local fabric shop next to one another. The variety of warmth and coolness in simple solid black is a wonderful exercise in understanding how much difference there can be in a warm or cool color of any kind.

Because we are usually working with more than solid fabric, it is important to note that most fabrics have other colors in them besides the main colorway. These accent colors also add or subtract from the overall warm feeling of the fabric. As you examine the fabric itself, train your eye to look at all the colors in a particular fabric. Are the little diamonds in the back white or cream? Is the green a soft apple green or a strong forest green with a bluish tint? As your eye begins to see all of the smaller aspects of each fabric, you begin to recognize the warm fabrics from the cool ones, and you can see the basis of how I use color in my work.

Finding Inspiration

So now you have begun to understand what you like, you know how to find a warm color palette at your local fabric shop, and you are ready for some fabric picking! For me a particular color combination or inspiration is where I always start. I choose a palette that I want to work with before I choose the fabrics or even walk into the store. For me the color comes first, and the rest falls into place.

The soft, yet vibrant, color combinations of old packaging labels, travel posters, and vintage illustrations from the late 1800s to mid-1900s have always fascinated me. I collect fruit labels, travel posters, European holiday postcards, children's illustrations, and the list continues. For whatever reason, we don't often put together such rich, saturated, and unusual color combinations in this day and age. We have moved to much cleaner, brighter, or more muted color palettes and lost many of those earlier looks and feels. If you look at vintage children's book illustrations, you will notice that the artist often chose colors that were just a little bit "off," as we would say today—not the color combination that you might expect to see. Chocolate with tomato red and buttercream, tangerine with aqua, chartreuse with golden yellow and plum—it makes me want to sew just writing about it! When I put palettes together, I love to try to capture that vintage feel that often seems so elusive today. I refer to these colors and palettes as "forgotten" colors because there is just something about them that makes me feel like I'm traveling back to another time. I create most of my fabric collections and sewn projects based on these color stories, and I hope that they transport you as they do me.

Fresh Vintage™ Color and What It Means

As I have worked with this particular color story for more than ten years of design and sewing work, I have come to refer to it as Fresh Vintage. Whether I am talking simply about Fresh Vintage color palettes or collections or the style that comes with that nostalgic love of old color and form, Fresh Vintage has

seemed like a wonderful way to name what I am talking about. Along with the colors and the design comes a love for flea markets and cast-off items. Many a fabric collection has started off with a chipped porcelain plate from the earlier 20th century or an old forgotten quilt top from the late 1800s. My husband often laughs and tells me that I was born in the wrong era, and my in-laws just don't understand my fascination with "old things"! But I think there is a beauty in these palettes and objects that we can learn from and work with to decorate our homes, create gifts for our friends, and, in general, make our lives more beautiful.

Adding Instant Vintage through Fabric and Design

As you start down the path of working with these palettes from my collections or ones of your own choosing and creation, you will find that there are certain types of fabrics or colors that will help you along your journey every time.

Yellow

First, I would like to share with you that yellow goes with everything! Many years ago, I heard another designer say this in a workshop on brights and contemporary fabrics. The same principle has translated very well into vintage color combinations. There is no color on the color wheel that looks bad with yellow. Think about it: Many of the most classic color combinations are paired with yellow—yellow/blue, yellow/purple, yellow/green—and yet somehow many people seem to be afraid of this wonderful color. I really don't know why that is, but you will quickly notice my love of yellow throughout the body of my work. Now, of course the yellow I am referring to is a soft, butter yellow or a warm, mustard yellow or a strong, cream yellow; no neons or primary colors here. These yellows often form the basis of the color palettes I work with. The strength of the yellow depends on what type of a feeling I am trying to convey or what type of a color combination I am trying to create.

Grounding Colors

Second, there are certain colors that will almost automatically ground or give depth to a color palette. Most quilters stay within the "medium" range of tones, never branching out into the true "lights" or true "darks" on the color spectrum. I have heard this fact over and over again in classes and workshops throughout my career. Personally, I have never struggled with adding cream and ivory as my "lights" but adding darks has been another story altogether. As I create my palette, I naturally start with the colors that are my intuitive favorites. Because the dark colors are not my favorites, I have needed to learn to add them into my projects to add visual interest to the end result. Incorporating dark browns, warm blacks, deep plums, taupes, and soft grays has added a strong grounding element to many of my designs. I have come to love these darker, dank colors for the amazing design element that they bring. These colors give your eye somewhere to rest as they move around the myriad other colors in your project. They absorb some of the intensity of other colors, and they provide a foil or a contrast to many of the medium tones that are sure to be in your palette. Not only will they help to give your overall project a more vintage, aged feeling, but they will round out your entire color palette, which will in turn strengthen the other color choices you have made. You will be amazed at what a few well-placed taupes or browns can add to an otherwise medium-toned quilt! On the flip side, you will be amazed at how much you miss these grounding colors and how flat your project might feel when you remove them. Again, this is an exercise that is worth trying if you are training your eye to work with color.

A side note that I thought I might share is that this principle has proven to work quite well in my home decorating ventures as well. As my decorating tastes and style have evolved, I've noticed that the simple placement of small black accents to my otherwise fairly neutral background palette made a huge overall difference in how much I liked the finished look. Small black knobs, ironwork, or artwork added a whole new dimension to both the neutrals and the color palettes in my rooms. The same can be said of adding natural or aged wood, wicker, or basket elements to a mostly cream or neutral room. You will notice an almost instant change with some of those simple additions. As a person who likes to decorate with large neutral backdrops and huge doses of color, these grounding colors have been a great addition to my home.

The Instant Vintage Fabrics

When working to create a fabric palette, especially when choosing for a quilt or a project that will have a lot of different fabrics in it, there are certain fabrics that I recommend adding to achieve that "instant vintage" that we are often looking for.

One of the easiest ways to achieve this feel is to add ginghams, stripes, and checks of any kind. Adding these small geometric prints to a palette that is otherwise filled with more organic or floral prints adds a great vintage feel. Dots of any kind or size add the same flavor. The simple, nostalgic feel of dot fabrics adds something special just by being present. Lastly, cutting up a large floral print has a similar effect. Whereas most people tend to keep a large floral print intact and place it on the border of a quilt or in a prominent place throughout the project, I recommend that you experiment with cutting up a large floral fabric so that each piece will sparkle with a different portion of the overall pattern. It is what our foremothers had to do out of necessity. We can choose to do it to help achieve the same unplanned, vintage look to our projects.

Linen

Linen is something you will definitely notice sprinkled throughout the book and something that I love adding into my designs. I originally fell in love with the look of natural linen when I was growing up in Poland as it was a fabric that was used often. At the time, I did not realize that Poland was a large manufacturer of linens (I believe it still is today). More recently, I have come to love and appreciate the feel of modern Japanese handwork and quilting. Natural colored linen is often featured in their work and mixed with vibrant and soft colors alike for absolutely stunning results. It is the Japanese inspiration that encouraged me to try mixing natural and taupe tones of linen with many of my own collections. As you can see, I have loved the results and think that linen can now officially be added as one of my grounding fabrics as well as a fabric that gives "instant vintage."

Proportion

When working with a variety of fabrics, it is very important to vary the proportion or scale of the various fabrics so that your eye has something interesting to look at. A project where all the fabrics choices are more or less of the same size and style will not be nearly as interesting as one where you have mixed large scale florals with little dots, stripes, medium florals, and everything in between. On another note, if you are working to reproduce a color palette that you have fallen in love with, remember to keep the color proportions the same. A mostly aqua project with a hint of tangerine feels completely different than a tangerine quilt with a tiny pop of aqua. The proportion of each color should stay the same as your original inspiration object to keep the same feel.

Creating a Palette That Works for You

Using all of the information provided here is an ongoing process—just like learning to sew or quilt—so please do not feel like you need to take it all in at once, especially if this is an area that is new to you. If you're an old hat with color then feel free to incorporate it all into your first project! For the rest of you, return to this chapter when you are stuck or unsure about the colors you are working with to see if perhaps some piece of advice here might strike you anew.

Taking whichever principles you want to heart, here are a few good places to begin in terms of color and design as you think about what you might like to work on first and what kind of an effect you want with your end product.

Neutral with a Pop of Color

One of the most effective ways to use color is simply as an accent. Creating an overall soft or neural palette and then adding dashes of warm and vibrant color is the way I most often decorate in my home. It is also the way I usually dress. Over the years, many of my favorite quilt projects have been the ones that have used a primarily neutral palette with dashes of one of my favorite colors, such as red, orange, or aqua. The Maison Blossom quilt is a good example of this idea, as is the Cherry Blossom quilt, although that falls a bit more into the two-color project category.

Star of the Show

Sometimes you have fallen in love with a particular fabric. One beautiful, vibrant piece of loveliness has made your heart beat faster. This is the type of fabric you want to feature as the star of your show. I do not recommend cutting this fabric up into a hundred little pieces and mixing it in a scrappy project because it will get lost in the overall color story that all those fabrics will be telling. Instead make an item that you might wear or carry around, such as an apron or bag, or find a simple, graphic quilt design that can utilize one to three fabrics well. Choose one or two supporting fabrics, perhaps even just a cream solid or small print, so that you can showcase your love.

A Fresh Vintage Palette

Creating a background of various cream prints coupled with a palette of several of those forgotten colors I discussed earlier is perhaps my favorite way to design a project, especially a quilt. I love

to use a large variety of fabrics to create the palette, and I live to play with stacks of fabric to see how the prints and colors interact with each other as they get moved around and rearranged. It is heaven to me! Of course, two-color quilts can be absolutely beautiful to look at. But scrappy quilts like the Basket Runner or the Summer House patchwork are my ultimate favorites.

A Riot of Color

Once in awhile, especially in the middle of the summer or when I am dreaming of those warm summer months, I want a project that is bathed and saturated in color and hits you with a pure riot of color right off! Summer Soiree and Tagalong Sister were just what I was looking for on those warm summer afternoons in California. The entire palette of fabrics creates the overall feel of the quilt with no single fabric standing out from another. This is definitely as bright and crazy as I go!

Time for Your Story

So you have read diligently through the previous basics chapters, have thought about your color sense, and know what kind of a palette you want to work with. Perhaps you already have your fabric stack ready and waiting to be cut into! However, despite your desire to get started, you might feel a bit overwhelmed about knowing where to begin. I know that sometimes jumping in is the scariest step of the journey! If you don't have this problem then you are probably not reading this section and are instead already sewing! For the rest of us, I strongly recommend that you start with something that feels simple to you—something doable. I think that a successful finish on an easy project usually gives us the confidence we need to tackle something new or more challenging. Often this process of building on our own strengths is the best route to learning a new craft. So, start with what you know!

As you work through the book, I hope that you find that it is full of projects that are familiar and comfortable as well projects that can challenge you with a new technique or method. I hope that that in the end you make them all. The projects that follow are not meant to be done in a progression but are options depending on your experience and your desire to try something new.

Chapter 5

Sewing to Add Handmade into Our Lives

For those of you who are sewers at heart, you should find yourself quite familiar and at home with many of the methods and techniques used in this chapter. Every project is meant to be a fairly simple and straightforward item that is easy to adapt to your own style or personal sense of home décor. Every project can be made in a weekend, if not an afternoon, for you or your family to enjoy for months and years to come! For those of you just starting out on your sewing journey, this collection of items serves as a wonderful way for you to familiarize yourself with some of the basics that we covered in the sewing chapter. Starting with the very selection of the fabrics that you will use, these projects are meant to bring some fabric joy into your daily living and give you a chance to bring your own sense of whimsy and personality into both your home and your wardrobe.

Fresh Linen Basket Liners

Fresh Linen Basket Liners

Finished Measurements: Varies according to basket size.
Samples shown: wire basket—8½" × 13"; wicker
basket—14½" × 19½" × 12"

I don't know about you, but we use baskets for everything in our
home. I think it's my way of organizing things in a decorative way
but still having the contents accessible to everyone for daily use. One
of my favorite ways to freshen up a room, other than the pillow
obsession I mention elsewhere in the book, is to add new liners to the
baskets that seem to single-handedly keep our house in order! This
pattern works for any size basket—from very large to tiny—and it
gives a fresh look to any room.

MATERIALS LIST

(9) ⅛ yards of various
cream fabrics. The yard-
age you need depends on
the size of your basket.

1¼ yards total (or less) for
the backside of the basket
liner (this will accommodate
a large basket); this can
be one fabric or a variety
depending on your choice.

1 yard twill tape (optional
for basket ties).

Measuring & Cutting Instructions

Given that every basket out there is a little bit different you need
to take some of your own measurements and follow my formula
in order to make your own basket liners. The instructions are
fairly straightforward and intuitive, and, if you just follow them
step by step, you will be on your way to beautiful new baskets
before you know it.

1. Measure the perimeter of the top of your basket. Add 2" to
   that measurement (1" for your seam allowance and 1" for
   ease of turning the top of your liner when finished). This is
   your length.

2. Measure the inside of your basket
   from top to bottom and add 3½"
   for the overhang. This is your width.

3. Cut as many 4" × your width strips
   as you need to cover your length. If
   the total of your strips is a bit over
   your length, that is fine. Sew them
   together to form the side of your

4 Top Sides = Perimeter
Your measurement + 2" = Your Length

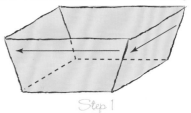

Step 1

Your measurement + 3½" = Your Width

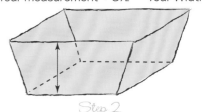

Step 2

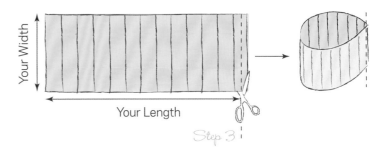

Your Width

Your Length

Step 3

basket liner. Measure your pieced strip and trim off the excess so that it equals your length. Sew the two short ends together to make a tube, RST.

4. Cut a piece of lining at the size you need (your width × your length). Sew it together to make a tube, RST. Set aside.

5. Measure the bottom perimeter of your basket. If your basket is a square or rectangle, you're good to go and you don't need to worry about making any of the tucks or alterations that the rest of us have to! However, most baskets angle inward and the bottom is either a bit or a lot smaller than the top. Measure around the four sides of your basket bottom. Add 1" to that measurement. This is your bottom size. Cut (2) bottom pieces and set aside.

6. Here is the math. Subtract the bottom perimeter number from the top perimeter number and divide that number by 4. Your result is how much you need to tuck in at each corner. The tuck you make will actually be half of that number because it will be tucked in half.

   For example, let's say that your top number is 53" and your bottom number is 41". 53" - 41" = 12" divided by the 4 corners = 3" per corner. You will tuck a total of 3" of fabric at each corner, or 1½" on each side of your tuck fold.

7. Start with one corner—it can be anywhere along your tube—and take one tuck the amount that is your number from Step 6. For the sample it was 3", or a tuck of 1½". Mark the spot with a pin and sew up 2" on that spot. Pin the tuck flat to make an inverted pleat of sorts.

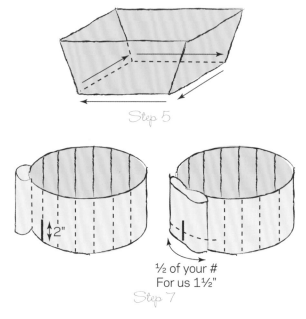

Your measurement + 1" = Your bottom size

Step 5

½ of your #
For us 1½"

Step 7

8. Measure over the length of one of your sides and mark with a pin. Add the number that you are tucking and mark with another pin. For the sample it was a 10" bottom side plus the 3" that were being tucked. Bring the two pin marks together and sew up that mark 2" as you did before. Repeat for the following two corners as well.

NOTE: If your basket is a square, all four sides will be the same. If your basket is a rectangle, you will have two sides of two different lengths when measuring, so don't get confused!

9. Because you will be piecing the bottom into this piece, cut a slit in the seam of each corner approximately ¼" to ⅜" long in order to help your corners spread when you match it to the bottom of the liner.

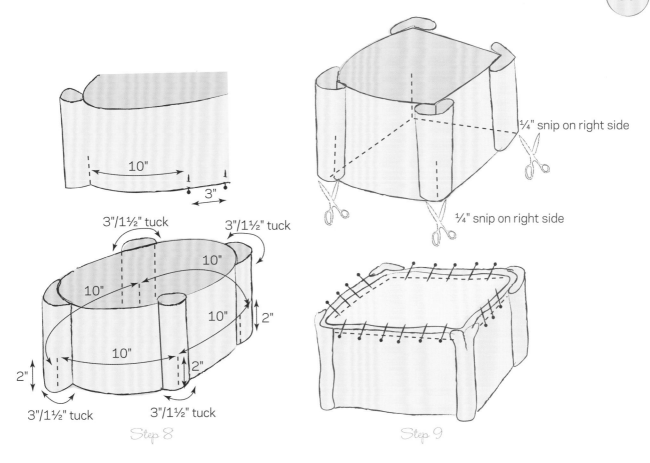

10"

3"

¼" snip on right side

¼" snip on right side

3"/1½" tuck   3"/1½" tuck

10"

10"

10"

10"   2"

2"

10"   2"

2"

3"/1½" tuck   3"/1½" tuck

Step 8

Step 9

Snip on the right side of the liner only and avoid snipping the pleats tucked on the wrong side of the liner corners. Place the lining piece RST with the bottom liner piece and pin together well. Sew the two together from corner to corner, continuing all the way around. Be sure to stop and pivot at each corner.

10. Make the lining in the same way. I chose to make the lining all from one fabric, but you can, of course, make both sides scrappy, especially for any basket that is see through like the metal one shown.

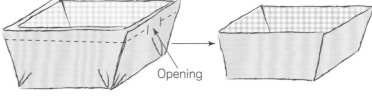

Opening

Step 11

11. Place the pieced liner "inside" the plain lining RST and pin together along the top. Sew the liners together along the top, leaving a 5" opening for turning. Turn RSO, press well, and place in your basket. Cuff around the outside of the basket.

Variations

1. As in our wire basket, there might be a loop or side handle or a label that you want to protrude from your liner. After you have fitted your finished liner into your basket, find the spot that you want to have visible and mark with a pin. Cut a small slit in that spot and simply zigzag or buttonhole the spot all the way around it to finish it off. Place the liner back on the basket, fitting the item through the hole.

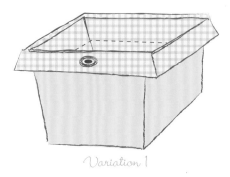

Variation 1

2. As in my large basket, many baskets have handles along the top. When you are finished with the liner but before you sew the

opening closed, make sure that the liner is still RST and fit the lining onto your basket to find the exact location of the handles or other openings. Mark both sides of each handle with a pin. If the handles are thick, be sure to mark both sides instead of just the center of each handle. Trace around the mark ½" in each direction (more if your handles are really chunky and wide) and at least 4" up into the liner. I am assuming a 3" overhang more or

less, so if your overhang is different take that into consideration when making this mark. Pin in place and snip down the middle of that shape, taking care to not snip all the way into the line on the end—stop at least ¼" short. Sew on the marked line all the way around for each side of each handle. Trim out the excess fabric on the inside, clipping the curve a tiny bit if necessary. Note that if you want to add pieces of twill tape for tying the basket like we did on our large wicker basket, you need to cut and insert those after you have measured and snipped your handle holes but before you have sewn them all the way around. Simply tuck them inside each side of each slit before you sew on your marked

lines. You need four lengths of at least 8" of twill tape. After you have finished the liner, position the handle cutouts around your handle and tie the tape into bows to close the liner onto the basket.

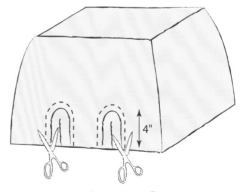

Variation 2

Vintage Bloom Pin

Vintage Bloom Pin

Finished Size: 3½" × 3½"

Sometimes it's those last minute embellishments that really make a simple project special. These little pins have served that purpose on many an occasion both in the studio and at home. I have used them on the Audrey Bags to give each one a little added personality. My daughter has used them to dress up her favorite plain shirts. I have used them as gifts for teachers and friends, and I am currently making up a whole set to decorate the curtains in my daughter's bedroom. Choose the tighter formation of the petals for a smaller feel or the wider set apart petals for a more airy-feeling bloom. Either way, these simple little embellishments can literally go with you anywhere!

MATERIALS LIST

⅛ yard flower fabric

⅛ yard flannel

⅞" or 1⅛" button form

Scrap of felt

Safety pin

Glue gun

Cutting Instructions

- From the flower fabric cut (11) 3" squares.
- From the flannel (or any other soft, thick fabric) cut (5) 3" squares.
- From the felt cut (1) 1½" circle template.

Assembly Instructions

1. Place two flower fabric squares together, RST. Place a flannel square on top. The flannel layer gives the petal a bit more body and form.
2. Use freezer paper to cut out a petal template. Press it to the square sandwich.
3. Remembering to backstitch at the beginning and end, sew along the petal template, taking care to sew a nice curved line. If your stitch line is jagged here you will have jagged petals, so take your time. Peel off the petal template and press it to another square sandwich to repeat the process. Make five petals total.

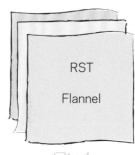

RST

Flannel

Step 1

Step 3

4. Cut out the petal with a scant ¼" seam allowance around the curve. Snip in a few spots around the top curve.

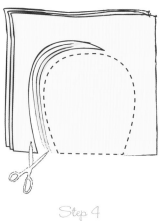

Step 4

5. Turn the petals RSO with a hemostat or other turning device. Press out with your finger or pressing bar and then press with your iron to get a nice, smooth petal shape.

6. Fold the petal in half and sew down ½", approximately ⅛" over from the fold. Press the seam flat. Repeat for all five petals.

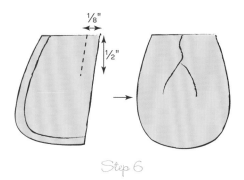

⅛"

½"

Step 6

7. Arrange the petals around the felt circle, overlapping the ends in the center. You can create different shaped flowers in this

step depending on how much you overlap the petals in the middle of the circle.

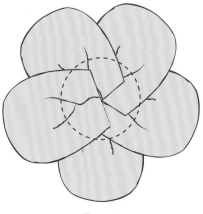

Step 7

DESIGN HINT: If you place your petals a bit further out, they will have spaces between them and look a bit more like a daisy. If you place them on top of one another in the center (don't worry about the bulk in the center), the petals will overlap one another much more and form more of a buttercup-type bloom. If you are unsure of what your flower will look like, place the button you will be using in the center to help you visualize the finished flower.

8. When you are happy with the layout, use the glue gun to glue the petals to the felt circle, one at a time. Be careful to not burn yourself and not use too much glue. A little goes a long way with a glue gun!

9. Make the covered button of your choice (I used both ⅞" and 1⅛" buttons on the sample flowers for different looks) and press the button shank to one side with the palm of your hand or the edge of your scissors so that the button lays flat on top of the petals. Glue the button to the center.

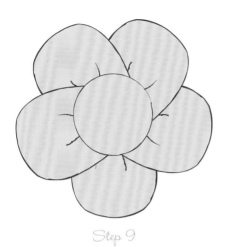

Step 9

10. Attach a small safety pin to the back of the bloom if you are going to add it to the Audrey bag. You can also add this pin to many other things, including your shirt or sweater, a little girl's dress, a belt, or any other purse. If you don't ever plan on taking if off the purse, feel free to stitch it on instead of pinning it.

The Audrey Bag

The Audrey Bag

I guess I should confess that although I am not much of a shoe girl, I am most definitely a bag lady! When I add the facts that I love both leather and handmade fabric bags of every size, I realize I might have a little bit of a problem. These dainty, romantic little bags are perfect for a date or just a day out on the town with your girl-friends. The little embellishment and the optional leather handles add something quite charming. The main size is perfect for any day, and the little one is just irresistible when all you need is something for your keys and a couple of credit cards!

MATERIALS LIST

½ yard fabric for body of bag

½ yard fabric for lining of bag

½ yard fusible fleece

Leather handles in 16", or make your own matching handle from leftovers from your bag fabric (optional)

Cutting Instructions

- From the main bag fabric cut (2) bag shapes for the size bag you are making. Both a large and a small template are provided.
- From the main bag fabric cut (1) 4" × 22" binding piece.
- From the lining fabric cut (2) bag shapes for the size bag you are making.
- From the fleece cut (2) bag shapes for the size bag you are making.

Assembly Instructions

1. Press the fleece to the wrong side of each piece of bag fabric. Press from the fabric side to ensure good adhesion.
2. Find the center by folding the bag piece in half, RST. Mark with a pin. You will be working on the fleece side. Measure over from the center 1" and mark it with a pin. Bring that pin in to meet the center pin. On the fleece side, sew along that center line where the pins meet, just ½" down to secure the pleat and keep it from moving. Open your fabric and repeat for the other side. Press the pleat in the back flat and pin it in place.

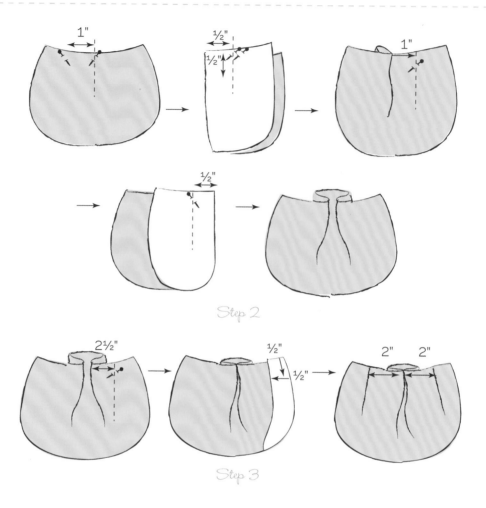

Step 2

Step 3

3. Measure over 2½" to the right and mark with a pin. Fold the fabric RST at the pin and measure over ½" from the fold and sew ½" down once again. Open the fabric back to the right. Repeat on the other side of the center pleat, 2½" to the left. You are making a half pleat on each side of the center inverted box pleat. Each half pleat should be approximately 2" away from the center pleat when done.

4. Repeat the pleat-and-tuck process on the remaining bag back piece.

5. Place the two bag pieces RST and pin all the way around the body of the bag. Sew together using a ½" seam allowance. Turn RSO and press the shape well with your fingers and the iron.

6. To make the lining, sew the two lining pieces together all the way around the body, RST, leaving the top open. Sew two basting stitches around the top of the lining bag, making sure you leave enough

thread on both ends with which to pull the gathers. Evenly gather the top of the lining bag until the opening is the same size as the opening on your outer bag.

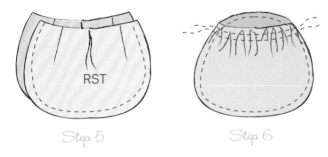

Step 5   Step 6

7. Place the lining, still RST, inside the outer bag. Pin the top raw edges of the lining to the top raw edges of the outer bag and baste them together with a ¼" seam allowance.

Step 7

8. Fold your 4" binding strip in half lengthwise, RSO. Draw a line ⅝" away from the raw edges on one side of the folded binding. This will be your sewing line. Leaving 3" of the end of the binding free, place the raw edges of the binding together with the raw edges of the outside of the bag. Pin in place. Remember to backstitch and sew the binding to the bag along the ⅝"

line all the way around the bag, stopping 3" away from the beginning.

Step 8

9. Fit the remaining free ends of the binding together to match the 3" opening and crease the pieces where they meet. Sew the two pieces together, using the creases as your sewing line. Trim off the excess fabric. Position the binding back onto the bag and continue your ⅝" sewing line to finish attaching the binding. Remove all pins.

Step 9

10. Turn the binding over the top and bind inside the bag by whip-stitching it to the lining by hand.

11. Add the leather handles to the outer sides of the top of the bag, placing them just to the outside of each outer half pleat. Stitch them on by hand.

12. To make your own handle, from a scrap of your bag fabric, cut two 2¼" x 8½" for the small bag and two 2¼" x 14" for the large bag. Fold the strip in half lengthwise RSO and press on the fold. Open the fabric again and press each side into the center fold. Open the pressed strip completely flat so that all three folds show. Fold each end under ½" and press to finish the ends.

½"   ½"

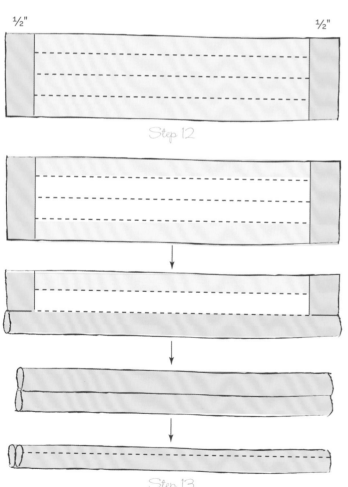

Step 12

Step 13

13. Cut three scraps of fusible fleece 1" x 7½" for the small bag and 1" x 13" for the large bag. Stack the fleece strips on top of one another and center them on the center fold. Fold each side back onto the fleece stack (the fabric edges meet in the middle) and press in place. Then fold it again so that the folded sides meet. Pin it together to make sure that the folds are even all the way down the length of your strip. Edge stitch along the folds, removing the pins as you go. When finished, roll the handles a bit to get a shape that's more round. Make sure you like the way they feel.

14. Attach the handmade handles to the inside of the bag, positioning them approximately ¾" down from the top or right on the bottom edge of your bag binding.

15. Attach the optional Vintage Bloom pin embellishment on the right side of the purse and take yourself out on a date!

Pin Cushion Buttercups

Pin Cushion Buttercups

Vintage Studio Style

Finished Dimensions: 2½" x 6½"

I have a serious thing for pincushions. I collect them with abandon and love every kind from those traditional old tomato pincushions to the most fanciful modern styles. Over the years I have designed many a pincushion pattern and yet I don't ever grow tired of making them or dreaming up new ones. To me there is a certain charm and something just a little bit different about every single one. This is a shape that I have wanted to do for quite some time—a big center with plenty of room and soft round petals shaping the outside. It makes me think of the little yellow woodland flower called a buttercup or a water lily floating on the small pond in our front yard.

MATERIALS LIST

¼ yard or fat quarter fabric for center

(1) charm pack or (6) scraps, fat quarters, or ⅛ yard fabric for the flower petals

⅛ yard green fabric for the leaves

Bag of stuffing

⅛ yard batting

Strong embroidery thread or thin yarn

Long needle

Cutting Instructions

- Cut (1) flower center
- Cut (2) center bottom pieces from center fabric
- Cut (12) petals in color pairs
- Cut (10) green leaves
- Cut (2) leaf bottom pieces from leaf fabric
- Cut (6) petal shapes and (5) leaf shapes from batting

Prep and Piecing Instructions

1. You need to turn under the edges of both the center bottoms and the leaf bottoms before you can use them. My favorite method is to press two layers of freezer paper together to make an extra thick piece, trace the template, and cut. Press the template to the center of your fabric circle. Turn the edges of the circle under using the starch method of appliqué (see Chapter 2) to get a perfect circle with turned-under edges. Prepare all four bottom circles in this way.

2. Place complementary petal pairs together, right sides facing each other, with a batting petal underneath. Pin together to prevent shifting. Sew the three layers together, leaving the bottom open. Repeat for each petal.

Step 2

3. Turn each petal right side out and press well to get a good outer seam. Hemostats might be helpful during this step to turn the petals RSO, if you have them. Topstitch each petal ¼" away from the edge.
4. Repeat the same process with the leaves. Be sure to pivot at the top of each leaf shape to get the point as you are sewing. Sew, turn, press, and topstitch the leaves.

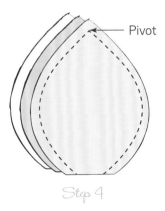

Pivot

Step 4

5. Lay thick embroidery thread or thin yarn ¼" away from the edge of the right side of the

center piece and machine sew a medium-sized zigzag over the yarn without ever stitching the actual yarn. Leave at least 6" of yarn on each end for ease of pulling.

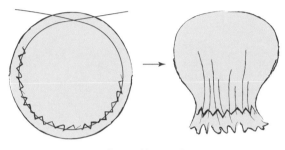

Steps 5 and 6

6. Pulling on both ends of the yarn, pull the ball partially closed. Stuff with the stuffing. When you think it is full, try to fill it some more! The more full you are able to get your center, the easier it will be to place pins in it. Don't worry if it doesn't close. In fact, it shouldn't close and if it can, you have not stuffed it full enough! Pull as closed as you can, tie the yarn off and tie the ends off. Close off the open bottom by placing the center bottom circle over it and hand-stitching it down to keep the batting inside.

Assembly Instructions

1. Lay out the petals around the center so that you can see about how they will look next to each other. Begin to hand-stitch the bottom of each petal to the bottom of the center ball, one petal at a time. Line up the bottom of each petal with the outside of that center circle. This will give you

nice, full petals that will overlap nicely. If you want petals that are a bit smaller or bend out less, then simply start stitching them on further down, closer to the center of the bottom. The petals will overlap one another on the sides regardless.

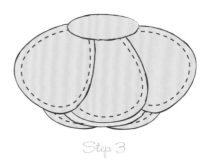

Step 3

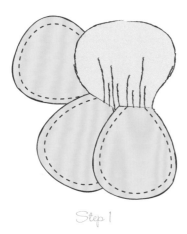

Step 1

2. When you have stitched all the petals to the ball (the petals are still flat at this point), begin to bring up, or "cup," each petal one at a time and hand-stitch it to the center approximately 1¼" from the end of each petal. Repeat for all the petals.

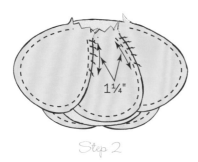

1¼"

Step 2

3. To close off the bottom, stitch the remaining center bottom piece to the bottom of the cushion.

4. To make the leaf set, lay out the five leaves in a circle slightly overlapping the inner ends so that they are all even. This is to give you a visual of about how much they need to overlap in order to form an even circle. Sew the first pair together on the bottom approximately ¼", just enough to secure them to one another. Sew another leaf to the first pair and so on. Connect the last two leaves. The leaves should lay flat. Hand-stitch a leaf center to the top and to the bottom to finish off the leaf set on both sides.

5. Attach the leaf set to the bottom of the pin cushion. Secure by hand-stitching to the center bottom. I also recommend hand-stitching it approximately ¼" from where the leaves start for a more secure bottom. Add pins and enjoy.

Steps 4 and 5

Dear Betty Apron

Dear Betty Apron

Doing Double Duty in the Kitchen

Finished Dimensions: One size fits most adults.
Child size 6-10.

I've owned many, many aprons in my life. Most of them have just hung on the hook and looked pretty. Some have been ugly but have been used a lot. When I started thinking of what kind of an apron I wanted to make, I realized that I wanted a cute apron that was comfortable, that adjusted at the neck and at the waist, and that covered me but still made me feel girly and retro! Inspired by an old flea market find, this apron is my version of the flirty '50s apron but with a little bit of body and use to it. It is fully reversible if you want to flip it over right before the company comes and show your "best side"! The cries of unfairness were too great, so when I finished the adult version I created a little-girl version as well.

MATERIALS LIST: ADULT SIZE

1¼ yards outer apron fabric

1 yard inner apron fabric

⅞ yard outer flounce fabric

⅞ yard inner flounce fabric, which can be the same or can coordinate with the outer flounce

⅝ yard binding fabric

MATERIALS LIST: CHILD SIZE

½ yard outer apron fabric

½ yard inner apron fabric

¾ yards outer flounce fabric

¾ yards inner flounce fabric, which can be the same or coordinate with the outer flounce

Cutting Instructions

- (1) apron from outer fabric (cut on the fold).
- (1) apron from inner fabric (cut on the fold).
- (2) neck ties and (2) neck ties reverse from outer fabric.
- (3) 3" × WOF strips. Piece the (3) strips for length. Cut into (2) 3" × 52" waist ties for the adult
  version. Cut (2) 2½" × 30" waist ties for the child version.
- (1) flounce from outer flounce fabric (cut on the fold).
- (1) flounce from inner flounce fabric (cut on the fold).
- 85" of 3"-wide bias binding (see the bias binding for adult version in Chapter 2).

SEWING TIP: The best way to cut is to place two layers of your fabric together, RST. Place the apron pattern on top and pin. With this method, when you cut out the neck tie, you are cutting (1) regular and (1) reverse automatically. Leave them together as they are ready for sewing as is.

Prep Instructions

1. Take a neck tie pair and pin them together, RST. Sew all the way around leaving the bottom open. Clip the corners and turn the neck tie tube RSO. Using hemostats in this step is a good idea. Press the tube well, rolling the seam edges out with your fingers to help push them all the way out to ensure an even press. Topstitch the neck tie all the way around. Repeat the process for the other neck tie as well.

2. To make the waist ties, fold each strip in half lengthwise RST to make a tube. Sew the end at a 45° angle and then stitch down the side. Leave the bottom open. Clip the corner and turn the tie tube RSO. It's a good idea to use hemostats in this step as well. Press the tube well, rolling the edge where the seam is to ensure an even press. Topstitch the waist ties all the way around. Repeat the process for the other waist tie as well.

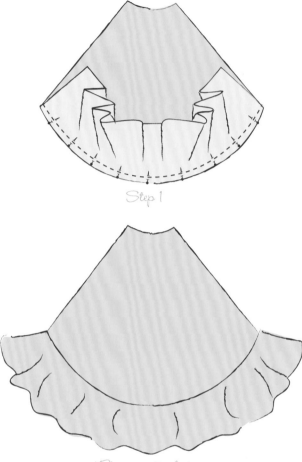

Step 1

Flounce attached

Assembly Instructions

1. Pin the flounce to the bottom of the apron. Start by pinning at each end and in the middle. Then continue to pin in between. Remember that the flounce is sewn at a different circular degree in order to create it. The two pieces are not meant to just lie flat on top of one another. Sew together with a ½" seam allowance, backstitching at both ends. Remove the pins and press well.

I've found that the best way to do this is to lift the main apron portion in the air, leaving the flounce portion on my ironing board. Press the flounce, a flat section at a time, the whole while holding the apron in the air. This ensures a nice press, with the seam going in the direction of the apron with minimal maneuvering. Topstitch the flounce.

2. Repeat Step 1 with the inner apron.

3. Measure 12" down each side and pin the waist ties on. (Note: See measurement variation at the end of the pattern.) Pin them toward the inside of the apron. This is a great place to adjust the pattern to fit exactly where your waist is or where you like to tie your ties. Adjust accordingly. Note*: see measurement variations at the end of pattern.

4. To pin the neckties to the top of the apron, measure ½" in from the edge, position your tie so that it's facing down into the apron, and pin in place. Make sure that you are placing the angled side of the tie toward the center. Stitch in place using a smaller seam allowance than what you are sewing with so that the seam does not show after the apron has been turned RSO. Repeat for the other tie.

5. Lay the two aprons RST and the ties tucked inside and out of the way of the seam. Sew together, leaving the apron open along the bottom of the flounce. Clip the corners and snip the curve of the neckline for smoother finish. Turn the entire apron RSO and press well.

6. Topstitch all the way around the entire apron.

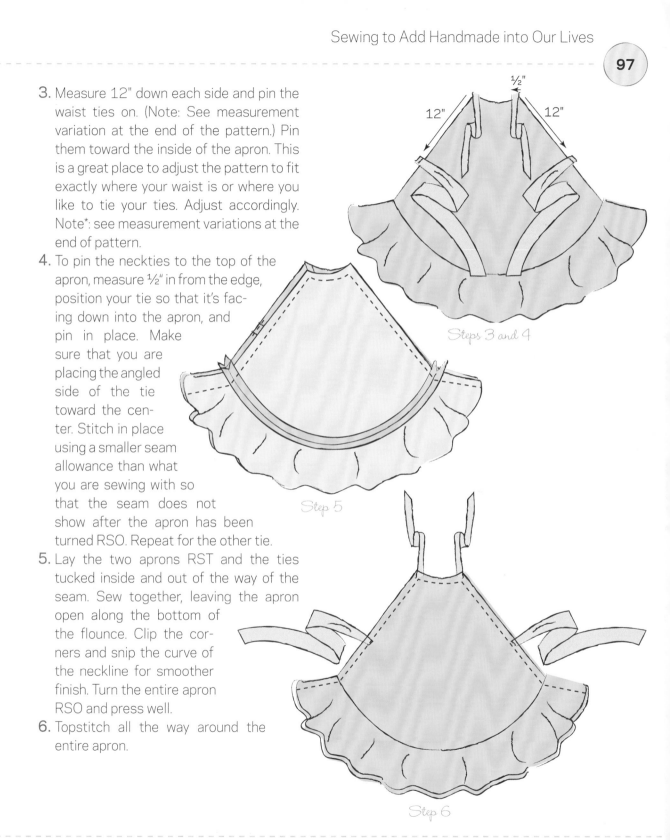

Steps 3 and 4

Step 5

Step 6

7. Bind the bottom of the flounce with bias binding. (Note: See the variation on the next page for the child's apron.) (For the sample, I thought it would look nice to have wider than the traditional ¼" binding so I sewed it with a ½" seam allowance instead.) Sew the binding to the outer apron and hand-stitch it to the inner apron. (Refer to Chapter 2 for information about adding binding.)

Variation

The child apron is assembled exactly the same way as the adult apron except that the ties need to be positioned 7½" from the top and that the bottom is not bound. When sewing the kid's apron, continue to sew all the way around the flounce, leaving a 6" opening along one side of the flounce for turning. Turn the apron RSO, turn the seam allowance of the flounce under, and edge stitch down.

Chapter 6

Dual **Projects**

Each of the projects in this chapter is meant to show you how far you can stretch yourself into the area that you are perhaps less familiar with. The projects in this chapter also demonstrate the inherent interconnectedness of sewing to quilting and vice versa. Even though most people seem to tend toward one or the other of these methods and crafts, it is not so far a stretch for us to venture out into the other. You can make each project using principles and materials of sewing or of quilting, and either method gives you equally pleasing results that appeal to either audience. Each project has its own charm and flavor depending on which method you choose and, of course, what fabrics you select for each item.

Directions for each project are given twice if the construction methods are completely different. Where the construction is quite similar regardless of which method you choose I've just noted the variations. This was probably the most fun section of the book for me to work on because not only was it a great lesson in contrast and working with one foot in each camp, but also it was a great opportunity to see the two crafts as sisters in the same family, so to speak.

Trio of Pillows: Saturday Morning Sham, All Dressed Up, Little Bloomers

Saturday Morning Sham

Classic Elegance

Finished Dimensions: 24" × 30"

I longingly admire designer pillow shams in catalogs and my favorite home stores and boutiques, but I seldom buy them as I always talk myself out of the purchase due to the price. A style that I seem to come back to again and again is the scalloped pillow with its lovely curves and delicate feel. So I thought it perfectly fitting to make one for this trio makeover. But be careful; these pillows are just a little bit addictive. I have made four, and I'm working on some more for my daughter's new "big girl" bed!

MATERIALS LIST

⅞ yard main sham fabric (front of pillow sham)

⅞ yard sham back fabric (back of pillow sham, which can be the same fabric as the main fabric or a coordinating print for more visual interest)

⅞ yard muslin backing (for quilted version only)

⅞ yard batting (for quilted version only)

⅞ yard fusible fleece (for sewn version only)

Freezer paper or tissue paper for pattern

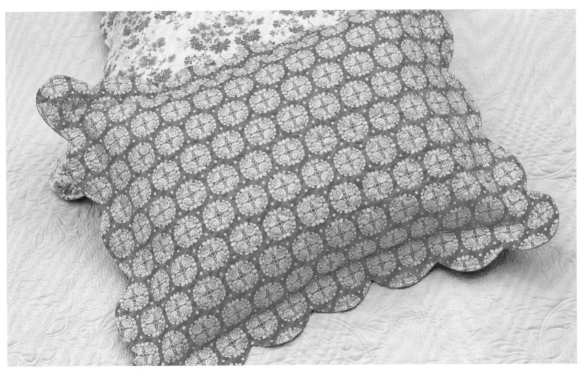

Saturday Morning Sham

Cutting Instructions for Sewn Sham

- From main sham fabric cut (1) 25½" × 31½" front piece.
- From fusible fleece cut (1) 25½" × 31½".
- From sham back fabric cut (1) 25½" strip. Cut into (2) 19" × 25½" back pieces.

Cutting Instructions for Quilted Sham

- From main sham fabric cut (1) 26½" × 32½" front piece.
- From muslin backing fabric cut (1) 28" × 34" backing piece.
- From batting cut (1) 28" × 34" piece.
- From sham back fabric cut (1) 25½" strip. Cut into (2) 19" × 25½" back pieces.

Piecing Instructions

DESIGN TIP: The only difference in construction on the quilted and sewn versions of all three of these pillows is that if you are making the quilted versions, you need to first quilt the main piece for each pillow. If you are making the sewn version, you first need to add either fusible fleece to the front of each pillow or use plain fabric.

If making the sewn version:

1. Press the main sham fabric. Make sure that you have pressed out any creases.

2. Press the fusible fleece to the back, lining it up exactly with the fabric square. To firmly fuse it to the fabric, turn the piece around and continue to press from the fabric side to fully adhere the fusible fleece.

If making the quilted version:

1. Make a quilt sandwich with the main fabric, the batting, and the muslin backing. Quilt as desired. I chose to do an all-over feather swirl design. I think that cross-hatching would also look wonderful on these shams.
2. Trim the quilted fabric down to 25½" × 31½". Lay aside.

For either version, continue with Step 3:

3. Finish one of the 25½" sides of each of the sham back pieces by turning the edge under ¼" and pressing. Then turn the same side under another ¾" and press again. Stitch the edge down, ⅛" away from the fold. Repeat for the other piece. You now have two back pieces, each with one finished edge.

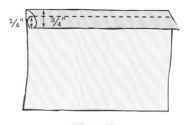

Step 3

4. Lay your front piece face up on your work surface and position the back pieces on top, RST, finished sides in the center. The back pieces need to line up with all of the outer edges of the front piece. The finished sides overlap one another in the center by approximately 5". Pin the back pieces to the front piece all the way around.

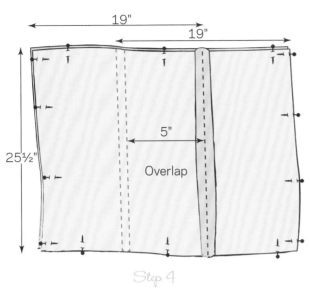

19"

19"

5"

Overlap

25½"

Step 4

6. Cut the scallops out all the way around with a ¼" seam allowance. Snip slightly into the scallop points.

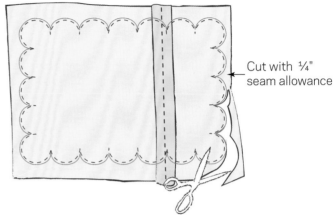

Cut with ¼" seam allowance

Step 6

5. Trace and cut out a scallop template from freezer or tissue paper. Center the paper template on your fabric sandwich and press it to the top. Sew right along the edge of the paper template all the way around. Peel off the paper template and remove the pins. If you prefer, you can trace the scallop line with a pencil, peel off the paper, and sew on the pencil line. If you are working with tissue paper, simply trace the line and proceed in the same manner.

3 clips into the point

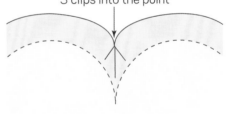

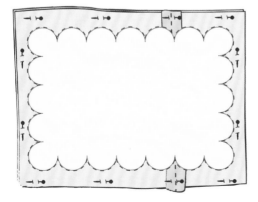

Step 5

Snipping in to scallop points

7. Turn the sham RSO. Work each scallop one at a time with your fingers and press, working on the front side the entire time. Topstitch all the way around the scallops, ¼" away from the edge.

8. Measure 1½" in from the edges and mark a rectangle with a soft chalk pencil or a disappearing marking pen. Sew on that line, taking care to make sure that the backing pieces are lying down flat and do not get caught in the seam.

DESIGN TIP: Often scallops get a bad reputation for being hard to do or at least hard to do right. I have found that if you clip the inner points and work the fabric to press nicely, you can get perfect scallops every time. Just be patient.

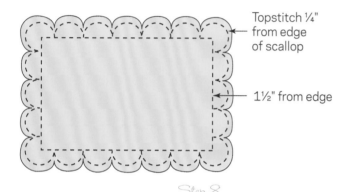

Topstitch ¼" from edge of scallop

1½" from edge

Step 8

9. Insert standard pillow form and make sure you pull it into the corners for a good fit.

All Dressed Up Pillow

All Dressed Up Pillow

Everything Is Lovelier with a Bow

Finished Dimensions: 25" × 25"

I love bows, and I love gifts and, well, I think we have already established that I love pillows! By sewing on a basic finished bow, a simple pillow cover becomes instantly sweet, charming, or sophisticated depending on the fabrics you choose. This is easily the most simple of the pillow trio and a wonderful way to spruce up any bed or couch.

MATERIALS LIST

1¼ yard pillow fabric

½ yard bow fabric

⅞ yard muslin backing (for quilted version only)

⅞ yard batting (for quilted version only)

26" square EURO pillow insert

Cutting Instructions for Sewn Pillow

- From pillow fabric cut (1) 25½" × WOF strip. Cut into (1) 25½" × 25½" front piece and (1) 16½" × 25½" back piece.
- From pillow fabric cut (1) 16½" × WOF strip. Cut into (1) 16½" × 25½" back piece.
- From bow fabric cut (2) 8" × WOF strips.

Cutting Instructions for Quilted Pillow

- From pillow fabric cut (1) 28" × WOF strip. Cut into (1) 28" × 28" front piece and (1) 16½" × 25½" back piece.
- From pillow fabric cut (1) 16½" × WOF strip. Cut into (1) 16½" × 25½" back piece.
- From backing fabric cut (1) 30" × 30" front square.
- From batting cut (1) 30" × 30" square.
- From bow fabric cut (2) 8" × WOF strips.

Piecing Instructions

If making the sewn version, simply proceed to Step 3 to begin.

If making the quilted version:

1. Make a quilt sandwich with the pillow front piece, the batting, and the muslin backing. Quilt as desired.

Given that the fabric has so much movement, I decided to quilt our standard all-over feather swirl design on the pillow front. If I had used a more plain fabric, a large double-feather wreath in the center of the pillow would add some gorgeous texture.

2. Trim the quilted front piece to 25½" × 25½". Set aside.

3. Finish one of the 25½" sides of each of the back pieces in the same manner as in Step 3 of the Saturday Morning Sham.

4. To make the bow, fold the strip in half lengthwise RST. Sew the strip shut with a 45° angle on the end and down the side. Trim off the excess fabric on the sewn diagonal end. Turn the fabric tube right side out through the open end, using your fingers or a hemostat. Press the seam well. Repeat for the remaining bow strip.

Step 4

5. Lay the pillow front piece face up on your work surface. Measure 8" down from the top and mark on the fabric with erasable marker. Find the center of the pillow and mark a spot 1½" over from the center on each side. Draw a line along the 8" mark all the way across the pillow front from the edge to each center mark. This leaves a center opening that is approximately 3" across. Line up your ties along the line, lining up the raw edges of the ties with the raw edges of the pillow front. Pin in place and sew the ties to the pillow front on

both top and bottom sides. Stop at each center mark and backstitch.

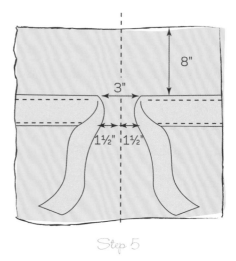

Step 5

6. Pin all the "free" ends of the ties in the center to keep them from being sewn into the seam in the next step. Position the back pieces on top RST. The back pieces need to line up with all of the outer edges of the front piece. They overlap one another in the center by approximately 5½". Pin the back pieces to the front piece.

Step 6

7. Sew the pillow shut all the way around, going through all the layers. Remove the pins and turn the pillow RSO. Push the seam out with your fingers all the way around, especially in the corners. Insert the EURO pillow form and tie the bow in the front.

Step 7

Little Bloomers Pillow

Little Bloomers Pillow

The Perfect Travel Companion

Finished Dimensions: 12" × 17" pillow plus ruffle

As a family we love to do getaways for an overnight or weekend. It helps us to reconnect, and traveling even just an hour away helps us to relax and slow down a bit. Hands down our favorite place to visit lately has been the Sonoma Valley. On a recent overnight, I walked into one of my favorite boutiques and saw these small linen travel pillows. I knew I had to make my own Fig Tree version.

MATERIALS LIST

⅝ yard main pillow fabric

⅝ yard ruffle fabric (can also be the same as main pillow fabric if preferred)

¾ yard muslin backing (for quilted version only)

¾ yard batting (for quilted version only)

12" × 16" pillow insert

Cutting Instructions for Sewn Pillow

- From pillow fabric cut (1) 18" × WOF strip. Cut into a 18" × 25" piece.
- From the ruffle fabric cut (2) 9" × WOF strips. Piece together for length and cut (1) 9" × 75" piece.
- From the ruffle fabric cut (1) 2" × WOF strip. Cut into (1) 2" × 26" facing strip.

Cutting Instructions for Quilted Pillow

- From the pillow fabric cut (1) 20" × WOF strip. Cut into a 20" × 27" piece.
- From the backing fabric cut (1) 22" × 29" piece.
- From the batting cut (1) 22" × 29" piece.

- From the ruffle fabric cut (2) 9" × WOF strips. Piece together for length and cut a 9" × 75" piece.
- From the ruffle fabric cut (1) 2" × WOF strip. Cut into 2" × 26" facing strip.

Piecing Instructions

If making the sewn version of this pillow, simply proceed to Step 3 to begin.

1. Make a quilt sandwich with the pillow front piece, the batting, and the muslin backing. Quilt as desired. I decided to quilt the same simple all-over feather swirl design to match the other pillows in the trio, but a cross-hatch or a simple channel stitch would add a lovely modern feel.
2. Trim the quilted fabric down to 18" × 25".
3. To make the ruffle, fold the 9" ruffle fabric in half lengthwise RSO and press. Follow the instructions in the box to make your ruffle.

Easy Gathering

To make a gather, all you need is a length of floss, pearl cotton, or string and an adjustable or large zigzag stitch on your machine. Place the string down the middle of your seam allowance space (approximately ½" in this case, so position the string approximately ¼" in from the edge of your fabric) and use a large zigzag stitch to topstitch back and forth over the string. Be sure to never stitch on the actual string. When you are done all you need to do is pull the string and voilà! The string never breaks. You can keep the string inside the gather when you're finished with the pillow assembly or pull it out if you prefer.

4. Pull the ruffle until it matches the length of your pillow front, 25" long. Smooth out the last ½" on each end so that it is flat. This will make sewing the ruffle together in the following steps much easier. Pin the ruffle to the right side of the pillow front with the ruffle lying against the pillow front and all the raw edges lined up together.

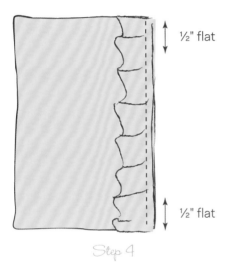

½" flat

½" flat

Step 4

5. Sew the ruffle to the pillow with a ½" seam allowance. Remove the pins and check that the ruffle is attached straight.

6. Turn down one long side of the facing piece ¼" and press. Sew down approximately ⅛" away from the fold.

Step 6

7. Leaving a ½" overhang at the beginning, place the raw edge side of the interfacing along the raw edges of the ruffle RST and pin in place along the entire ruffle. You should also end with a ½" overhang. Start sewing approximately 1½" from one end and sew on top of the ruffle, also stopping approximately 1½" away from the end. Make sure you are sewing a "smidge" over to the left from the ruffle seam so that the ruffle seam line does not show. Pin those "free" end pieces toward the inside of the pillow to avoid them being sewn into the seam in the next step.

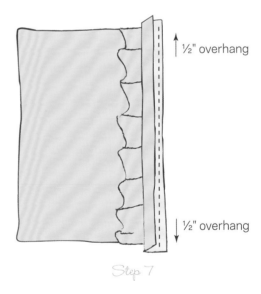

½" overhang

½" overhang

Step 7

8. Fold the pillow in half RST and line up the ends and side of the pillow and pin. Sew the pillow together along the two sides and all the way to the end of the ruffle. Be sure to backstitch well.

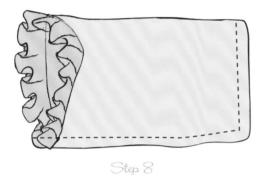

Step 8

9. Turn the pillow RSO and pull the ruffle out. Unpin the ends of the facing, lining up the "free" ends flat with the ruffle tube. Following the directions for single fold binding on p. 54 in Chapter 3, finish the ends of the facing strip. Trim any excess of the facing strips.

Step 9

10. Pull the finished unattached side of the facing over the raw ruffle edges and pin in place on the inside of the pillow tube. Sewing on the front side of the pillow, sew the facing to the inside of the pillow tube, thus attaching the facing, enclosing the ruffle's raw edges, and creating a finished stitch line on the right side of the pillow. Sew carefully and slowly to make sure you are catching the edge of the facing on the inside of the tube as you sew.

11. Insert a pillow form and pull it into the corners for a good fit.

Back-to-School Lunch Bag

Back-to-School Lunch Bag

Finished Dimensions: 7½" × 9½" for child version and 9" × 11" for "mama" version

As a family of five, we seem to go through an inordinate number of paper bags for lunches, projects, picnics, and the like. Over the years I have admired many different kinds of insulated and lunch look-alike bags, but I wanted one that looked and felt like a lunch bag complete with crisp edges, a flat bottom and turned-in sides. Mostly I wanted it to feel like me. I think this might be that bag. The design evolved a bit when my daughter asked me to add a strap so it would be easy to carry to the park. Of course I had to make a mama version and a kid version because that's just the way I roll around here!

MATERIALS LIST

Sewn Lunch Bag:

½ yard laminated cotton

2¼" piece of hook and loop tape

3¼" × 6¾" piece of card-board for kid version or 3¼" × 7¾" for mama version (optional)

Tissue paper (optional)

Cutting Instructions

- Cut (1) 12" × 33" main bag piece for kid version or 13" × 34½" piece for mama version.
- Cut (1) 3" × WOF strip for the strap.
- Cut (1) 7⅛" × 11" piece for bottom reinforcement for kid version or 7⅛" × 12" for mama version (optional).

Piecing Instructions

1. Starting with the main bag piece, mark 2¼" in on each long side with a light pencil line on the right side of the laminated cotton. Fold at that line and press. Always use a pressing cloth when pressing laminated cotton or oilcloth of any kind.

SEWING TIP: If your laminated cotton is sticking in your machine sew with a piece of tissue paper placed on the right side of the fabric. With this method you can see the edge of your fabric right through the tissue, and the tissue tears off at the end of your sewing. For more information on working with laminated cotton, see page 51 in Chapter 3.

2¼"

Fold, press, and topstitch

Steps 1 and 2

2. Edge stitch the fold. Repeat for the other long side.

3. Keeping the bag sides folded, fold one short end of the bag under ½" and then fold ½" again to create a finished edge. Topstitch the end down, approximately ⅛" away from the edge. This is the top of your bag flap.

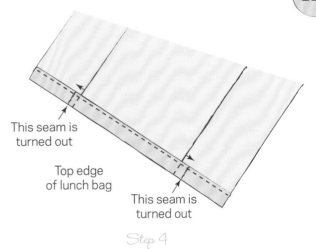

This seam is turned out

Top edge of lunch bag

This seam is turned out

Step 4

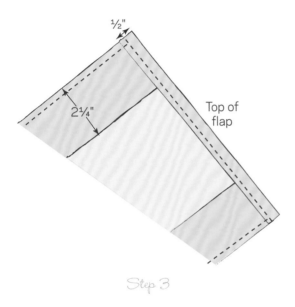

½"

2¼"

Top of flap

Step 3

4. Open the bag completely flat and fold the other short edge ½" and then ½" again to create a finished edge. Topstitch the end down on the folded edge, approximately ⅛" away from the edge. This is the top of your lunch bag. It is important that the 2¼" seam edges need to be turned toward the outsides.

5. Turn the bag over so right side is up. Keeping your bag open, measure 9½" down from the top of the flap (8½" for the Mama version). Mark lightly with a pencil on the edge of the right side. Repeat for the edge of the left side.

6. To make the strap, fold the strip more or less in thirds the long way, with the final fold not quite meeting the edge. Press well. Stitch ¼" in from each side. Your finished strap should be approximately 1" wide.

Top flap

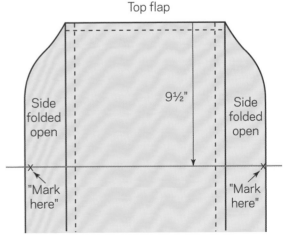

Side folded open

9½"

Side folded open

"Mark here"

"Mark here"

Step 5

7. Sew up the sides of your bag, sandwiching the strap between the two right sides, even with the *top edge* of the bag. Begin by laying your strap across the bag below the top *flap*, lining up one short raw edge of the strap at the mark you made in Step 5. The raw edge of the strap should be even with the raw edge of that 2¼" fold you made in Step 1. Carefully fold the top *edge* of the bag up, bringing the right sides of the fabric together, with the top *edge* lining up on top of the already-positioned strap. Sew up the side of the bag, being sure to backstitch to lock the seam at the top edge. Repeat on the opposite side, being sure the strap is not twisted inside.

8. Fold one bottom corner flat to form a triangle. Turn the bag triangle over, so the seam you created in Step 1 is on the top. Sew just to the right of that seam, being sure not to catch the inside folded edge in your new seam. Backstitch at both ends. Repeat on the other bottom corner.

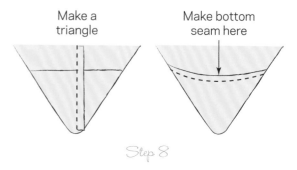

Make a triangle

Make bottom seam here

Step 8

9. Turn the bag right side out and fold the bottom flat, like a traditional lunch sack. Now, stitch along the very bottom edge in the front and the back, to give the bottom of the bag a finished look.

Top flap

Top flap

Strap raw edge →

9½"

Right side

← Strap tucked completely inside

Wrong side

Stitch the sides of bag closed

Step 7

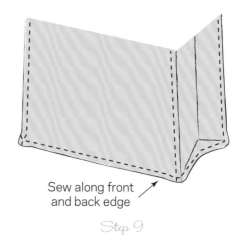

Sew along front and back edge

Step 9

and approximately 5½" down from the top of the bag.

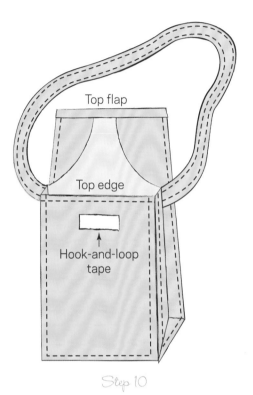

Top flap

Top edge

Hook-and-loop tape

Step 10

10. Roll down the top as little or as much as you like for your style. For the kid version, I rolled the flap several times and attached the hook and loop tape 5½" from the end of the flap and approximately 1" down from the top of the bag. On the mama version I placed the hook and loop tape approximately 1" from the end of the flap

11. To make the optional cardboard bottom, fold the bottom reinforcement fabric in half lengthwise RST and sew to create a tube. Turn RSO, press, and slip the cardboard into the tube. Scoot the fabric so the seam falls in the middle of the bottom of the cardboard. Turn the laminated cotton edges under and secure them on the bottom of the cardboard with a glue gun, a few hand stitches, or hook and loop tape. For a cotton fabric bottom, stitch the edges under instead to create finished sides.

Mama Too Quilted Lunch Bag

Finished Size: 9" × 11"

When the kid version was done, I decided that Mama needed one, too, so as to not feel left out. Actually my daughter, in all of her great six-year-old wisdom, decided on that!

MATERIALS LIST

½" yard quilted fabric

¼ yard cotton fabric that coordinates to quilted fabric

2" piece of hook and loop tape

(1) 3¼" × 7¾" piece of cardboard (optional)

Mama Too Quilted Lunch Bag

Cutting Instructions

- From quilted fabric cut (1) 14" × 35" strip.
- From coordinating fabric cut (1) 4¼" × WOF strip for the strap
- From coordinating fabric cut (1) 7⅛" × 12" for bottom reinforcement of bag (optional)

> **QUILTING HINT:** Given that you "lose" a lot more fabric when sewing with a thicker quilted piece I expanded the dimensions of this version just a bit to accommodate that. You can, of course, choose the laminated bag sizes for a somewhat thinner lunch bag profile.

1. Follow the piecing and assembly instructions for the laminated bag. When sewing the sides at the 2¼" mark, sew closer to a ¼" top stitch than the tiny edge stitch I recommended in the laminated cotton bag. It's just not possible to accurately sew such a small seam on quilted fabric. The same is true when you sew the bottom stitch in Step 9 in the previous instructions.

2. After you have sewn the two sides down, serge or satin stitch the raw edges all the way down. (This isn't necessary with the laminated cotton version because the edges of laminated cotton are finished and clean and don't need edging. With standard cotton, as is used here, the edges are raw and contain loose threads. You should finish them in some manner for a finished look.) After stitching, trim all the stray threads for a cleaner finish. If you want a completely finished bag inside then you can bind these edges. Just be careful to make a very skinny binding that will not interfere with these edges being stitched up the sides in the next step.

3. To make the strap, fold the strip in half lengthwise RSO and press well. Reopen the strip and fold and press each long side into the center to create three folds and four even sections. Refold the pressed strip in half and sew the two folded edges together, edge stitching them as you go. Edge stitch the other long side of the strap as well to create a finished look

4. Finish the bag according to the Back to School Lunch Bag instructions.

Boardwalk Beach Tote: Seaside Version

Boardwalk Beach Tote

I don't think I am exaggerating when I tell you that I have a different tote bag for every occasion—one for the beach, one for soccer practice, one for sewing class, one for the farmer's market—should I go on? So basically I couldn't leave this collection behind without adding a fabulous beach tote big enough for everything you might want to throw in it. It's perfect for picnicking, too. This tote is now officially my favorite, and I might just have to take it to sewing class, the market, and soccer practice!

Boardwalk Beach Tote: Seaside Version with Laminated Cotton

Cutting Instructions for Sewn Version

- From main bag fabric cut (2) 26" × 36" main bag pieces.
- From main bag fabric cut (1) 26" × WOF strip. Cut into (2) 19" × 26" pocket pieces.
- From flap fabric cut (1) 16" × WOF strip. Cut into (2) 16" × 18" pieces.
- From flap fabric cut (2) 8" × WOF strips for the strap.
- From fusible fleece cut (1) 16" × WOF strip. Cut into (2) 16" × 18" pieces.
- From fusible fleece cut (2) 2" × WOF strips.

NOTE: Although a bit trickier to work with than standard cotton, laminated cotton is well worth the effort! It makes for a perfect beach, lunch, or diaper bag given how easy it is to take care of and its durability. For more info on working with laminated cotton see page 51 in Chapter 3.

MATERIALS LIST

2½ yard laminated cotton, or 1⅜ yard outside fabric and 1⅜ yard inside bag fabric for the quilted version

1⅜ yard batting (quilted version only)

½ yard cotton flap fabric

½ yard cotton strap fabric

⅝ yard fusible fleece

¼ yard binding fabric (quilted version only)

1⅛" and 1½" button forms

1½" magnetic closure

Tissue paper

Piecing Instructions

1. Place the bag pieces together RST and sew along the 26" sides on the top and bottom. Turn RSO and press the top carefully through a cloth. Do the same thing with the pocket pieces along the 19" side. Using tissue paper on top, topstitch both 19" sides of the pocket.

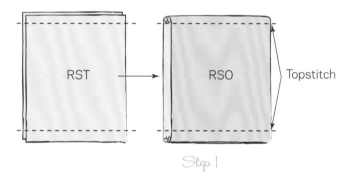

Step 1

2. Fold the pocket in half so that the 19" sides are together at the top. Pin the folded pocket to the left outside of the bag piece, starting 1" down from the top of the 26" side. Pin well along the left side. Baste the pocket to the bag with a ¼" seam.

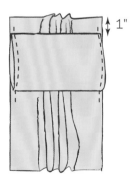

Steps 2 and 3

3. Attach the right side of the pocket to the bag. Note that the pocket is shorter and will not fit evenly across the bag piece. You need to scrunch the bag piece in the center in order to get the right pocket side to meet with the right side of the bag. Pin right side in place, also 1" down from the top. Pin and baste carefully together.

4. Fold the bag piece **behind** the pocket so that the 26" sides are together at the top and the pocket is facing you. Pin all the layers together on the left side. With a ½" seam allowance, sew all the way down the seam through all eight layers, continuing all the way down to the corner. Given the layers, sew slowly and carefully and backstitch far on both ends. Note that the bag piece extends past the bottom of the pocket as you sew. Repeat for the other side.

Step 4

5. Given that you are working with laminate, you don't need to finish the side seams, but for a nice finish I recommend zigzagging and pressing the seams open on both sides.

Step 5

6. Open the bottom of the bag in the same way as you did in the Back to School Lunch Bag and place the corner centered in front of you, making sure the zigzagged seam is pressed open. Measure 3½" on each side of the centered seam—7" across. Draw a line all the way across and pin in place. Sew along the drawn line, backstitching several times at the ends to stabilize the bottom of the bag. Take care to keep the bottom of the pocket piece out of the way of your sewing so that it does not get caught in your bottom seam. Trim the corner of the bag with a ½" seam allowance.

7. Repeat Step 6 for the other corner. Turn the bag RSO.

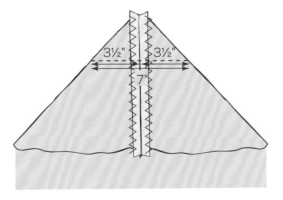

Steps 6 and 7

8. To make the flap, press a fusible fleece piece to the back of each flap piece. Press well from the fabric side for good adhesion. Find the center of one of the flap pieces by folding it in half lengthwise. Next measure 4" up from the bottom of the piece on the fold and mark that point with a pin. Place the male side of a magnet centered on that point, snip through the fabric and fleece and attach the magnet to the flap.

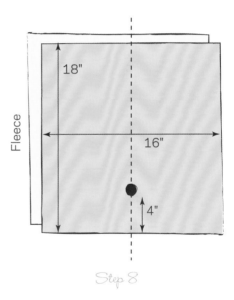

Step 8

9. Place the two flap pieces together, RST, fusible fleece sides out. Measure 3½" up and over on each bottom corner and mark. Remember that you are working on the fleece side so make sure your pieces and measurements are accurate. Trim the corners at those marks.

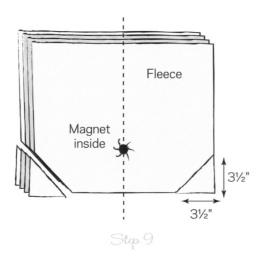

Fleece

Magnet
inside

3½"

3½"

Step 9

place. Mark 1" down on the flap and sew along that line all the way across the flap, backstitching several times at both ends.

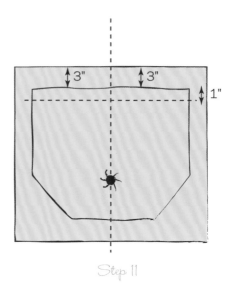

3" 3"

1"

Step 11

10. Keeping the flaps together, pin together. Sew on the three sides, leaving the top open. Trim the four corners a bit. Turn the flap RSO. Press well all the way around to ensure a good shape. Topstitch approximately ½" away from the edge.

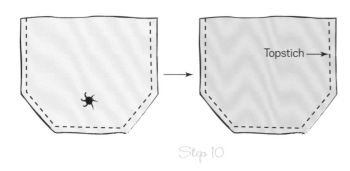

Topstich →

Step 10

11. Find the center of the back of the bag by folding it in half and marking with a pin. Find the center of the flap by folding it in half and marking with a pin. Measure 3" down from the top of the bag and mark with pins or a water soluble pen. Match the center of the flap with the center of the bag and line up on that 3" line. Pin in

12. Fold the flap up and over the top of the bag and press the seam well. Measure another 1¼" up the turned flap, pin in place, and sew along that line, backstitching at both ends.

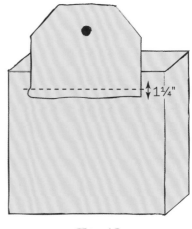

1¼"

Step 12

13. Find the center of the bag front and measure 6" down from the top. Mark with a pin. This should be where you place the flap magnet. Let the flap fall forward onto the front of the bag in order to check that the magnets will line up. If for some reason your flap has moved over during sewing, you can compensate here by moving the placement of the magnet over a bit to match. After you have determined your best location, place the female side of the magnet on that point and attach it to the bag.

side. Open the fabric again and press each side into the center fold. Open the pressed strip flat so that all three folds show. Place the fusible fleece strip on one of the inner sections and press in place. Fold each side back onto the fleece and press in place. Fold again so that the folded sides meet together.

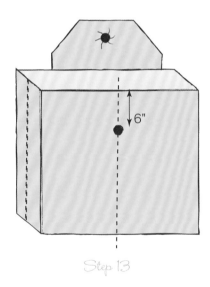

Step 13

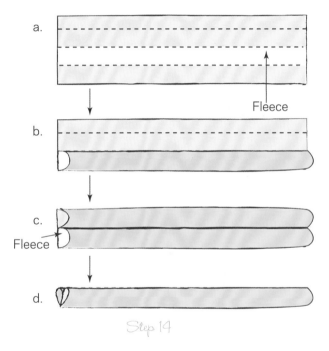

Step 14

14. To make the straps, fold the 8" strap piece in half lengthwise, RSO, and press on the fold. Trim off the selvedge ends on each

15. To make the angled ends, fold the ends inside out and pin them open in place. Mark the center of the strip ¼" down from the end and 1⅛" down on each side.

16. Sew from dot to center dot, to dot, back-stitching at both sides. Trim the excess fabric around the sewn line. Repeat for the other end of the strap. Turn the ends RSO and work to press the points out as well as you can.

17. Topstitch all the way around the strap approximately ⅛" away from the edge. Repeat to make a second strap.

18. Attach a strap to the front of the bag by lining it up right along the outside of where the flap falls, approximately 3½" down on each side. Stitch around the entire attached portion and then stitch an X through it in order to stabilize it. Repeat for the other side.

19. Attach the button to the center of the flap in front of the magnet and on the straps if desired. I used the 1½" size for the flap (Seaside version) and the 1⅛" size for the straps (Sunshine version).

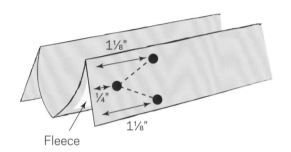

Steps 15 and 16

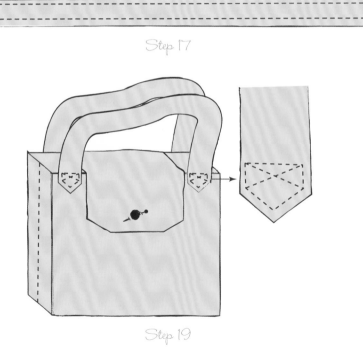

Step 17

Step 19

Boardwalk Beach Tote: Sunshine Version

Boardwalk Beach Tote: Sunshine Version with French Seam Finishing

Cutting Instructions

- From main bag fabric cut (1) 39" x 48" piece.
- From inside bag fabric cut (1) 40" x 49" piece.
- From batting cut (1) 40" x 49" piece.
- From flap fabric cut (1) 16" x WOF strip. Cut into (2) 16" x 18" pieces.
- From flap fabric cut (2) 8" x WOF strips for strap.
- From fusible fleece cut (1) 16" x WOF strip. Cut into (2) 16" x 18" pieces.
- From fusible fleece cut (2) 2" x WOF strips.
- From binding fabric cut (3) 2½" x WOF strips.

Piecing Instructions

1. Make a quilt sandwich with the main bag fabric, batting, and the inside bag fabric. Quilt as desired. Diana quilted her signature feather all-over design throughout the whole piece. From the quilted piece cut (1) 26" x WOF strip and cut into (1) 26" x 38" piece. Cut (1) 19" x WOF strip and cut into (1) 19" x 28" pocket piece.
2. Bind the two 19" edges of the pocket piece using one 2¼" binding strip. After the pocket is bound, fold it in half, matching the bound sides together, and pin along the top, RSO.

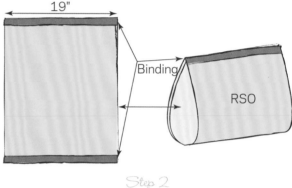

Step 2

3. Pin the folded pocket to the left inside of the bag piece, starting 1" down from the top. Pin well along the left side. Baste the pocket to the bag with a ¼" seam.
4. Attach the bound pocket in the same manner as in Steps 2 and 3 of the Seaside version.

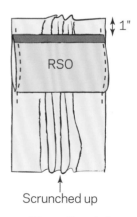

Scrunched up

Steps 3 and 4

5. Fold the bag piece **over** the pocket so that the 26" sides are together at the top. Pin all the layers together on the left side. Sew through all four layers using a ⅜" seam. Given the number of layers, sew slowly and backstitch on both ends. Note that the bag piece extends past the bottom of the pocket as you sew. Check the inside after you are done to make sure you caught all the layers. Repeat for the other side.

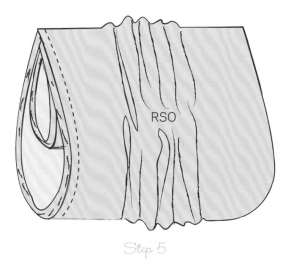

Step 5

6. Remove the pins, trim the seam allowance to ¼", and trim any stray threads so they don't get caught in the next step.
7. Turn the bag RST so that you have the pocket in front of you. Pull the pocket (both sides) in one direction and the bag (both sides) in the other. Press in this position well to try to get the best crease you can.

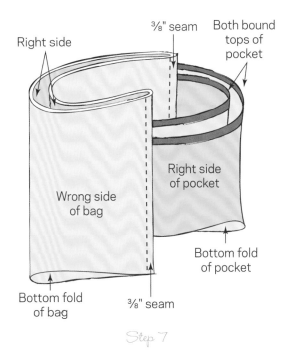

Step 7

8. With the fabric in this position, pull both sides taut in order to avoid any tucks or inconsistencies in the next step. With the fabric taut on both sides, sew *along the bag* seam, ⅜" away from the edge, enveloping the entire raw edge seam inside in the process. Sew from the top, through the four layers of the pocket, all the way to the bottom corner. Backstitch well on both ends. Repeat for the other side.

9. Turn your bag RSO and press the seam nicely. You now have a completely finished French seam on the inside of your bag.

10. Create the bottom of the bag in the same manner as in Step 6 and 7 of the Seaside version. In this version keep the corners intact and do not trim. Take extra care when sewing over the French seam due to its bulk, backstitching several times over the seam itself.

11. Turn the bag RSO and bind the top of the bag using two 2¼" binding strips.

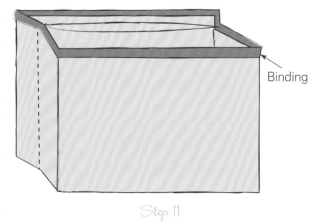

Binding

Step 11

12. Finish the bag as described in Steps 8 through 19 of the Seaside version.

Sweet & Scrappy Woven Floor Mats

Sweet & Scrappy Woven Floor Mats

Finished Size: Approximately 20½" x 26½"

Given the amount of sewing we do in our studio, sometimes I feel like we are drowning in scraps of every color and shape imaginable! When we are tired of making scrap bags for our website, we often still have piles of color-sorted yumminess, and I can't help but start planning out new projects. This time the scraps just looked like they needed to be woven mats! I had long wanted to make a mat out of fabric that somewhat resembled those crocheted fabric rugs that I see everywhere. Now the hardest thing is going to be deciding which room they will go in!

MATERIALS LIST

(11) various ¼ yards creams, pumpkins, or aquas. You can, of course, choose any other color grouping you like as well.

¾ yard for the back mat.

¾ yard fusible fleece or batting depending on the version (if you prefer, you can use pre-quilted fabric for the mat, in which case you need ¾ yard total and no back).

⅜ yard binding (quilted version only).

Sewn Version

Cutting Instructions

- From each fabric (choose cream, aqua, or pumpkin) cut (2) 4½" x WOF strips, for a total of (21) 4½" strips.
- From each fabric (choose cream, aqua, or pumpkin) cut (2) 19¾" x 25¾" back mat pieces.
- From fusible fleece cut (1) 19¾" x 25¾" piece.

Piecing Instructions

NOTE: I used a ¼" seam allowance for both versions of this mat.

1. Fold each strip in half lengthwise, RST. Sew shut along the long side, but leave both ends open.
2. Turn each tube RSO and press with the seam in the center of one side. This will be the back side of the tube. Repeat for all (21) strips.

Step 1

Step 2

3. To make the back mat, press the fusible fleece to the backside of a mat front piece. Press well. Place the remaining back mat piece on top of the sandwich, RST. Line up all the edges, pin in several places to secure and sew the three layers together, leaving a 5" opening on one side. Turn the mat RSO through the opening and press well. Close the opening and sew shut along the outer edge. Topstitch the mat all the way around with a ¼" seam allowance to create a finished edge.

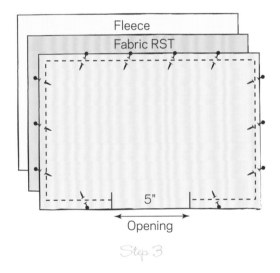

Step 3

4. Working on the top of the mat, begin to weave the strips on one corner. Make sure that the strip seams are facing down and that you have at least 3" hanging over the edge of the mat when you begin. Lay down one strip lengthwise and one crosswise. Lift each strip up in order to position the next one as if you were weaving a basket. Continue all the way up and across. You will need (12) strips across the width and

(9) strips from top to bottom. As you weave, make sure that you are scooting the strips close to one another as you go. If you leave gaps between the strips, they will not fit all the way across your mat.

Step 4

5. After you are done weaving, make sure that all your strips are straight and that you still have at least 3" hanging over on all sides. You will have more than that on one side. Pin the entire layout to the mat itself. Trim the sides to a 3" overlap on the two long sides so that all four sides have a 3" overlap.

a.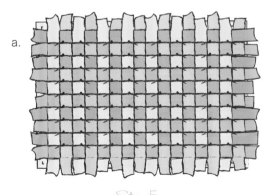

Step 5

6. As you begin to pin each strip, turn the end underneath the strip, making a loop. The loop itself should be 1¼". Make sure that the bottom of the loop is tucked in between the strip and the mat so that it gets sewn into the mat when you sew the perimeter. Continue tucking in the loops and pinning the strips all the way across the entire mat.

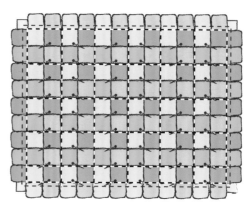

Steps 7 and 8

Step 6

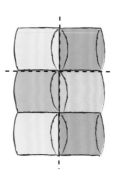

Close up of Step 8; stitches go along side folds and not on them

7. After you've pinned the mat, sew the loops closed all the way around the outside of the strips by sewing along the entire perimeter of the front of the mat. Make sure you are catching the edge of the back mat as you sew. If the mat has shifted over, tug it slightly back into place to make sure you are sewing the loops closed on top of the mat itself.

8. Continue to sew every other strip length-wise and crosswise to attach the strips to the mat itself. When sewing, sew along the pressed outer edges of each strip and not on them so that they still have move-ment after you are done sewing. What I mean by this is that you should still be able to put your finger all the way through the woven sections even after you have sewn them.

Quilted Version

Cutting Instructions

- From each fabric (choose cream, aqua, or pumpkin) cut (2) 4½" × WOF strips. Cut a total of (21) 4½" strips.
- From each fabric (choose cream, aqua, or pumpkin) cut (2) 21" × 27" back mat pieces.
- From the batting cut (1) 21" × 27" bat-ting piece.
- From the binding cut (3) 2¼" × WOF strips.

Piecing Instructions

1. Repeat Steps 1 and 2 from the sewn version of the mat.
2. To make the back mat, make a quilt sandwich with the mat fabric and the batting. Quilt as desired. I did a simple meander as the mat never shows on the front. Trim the piece to 18¾" × 24¾". Bind the mat using the (3) 2¼" binding strips.
3. Repeat Steps 4 through 7 of the sewn version of the mat.
4. On the quilted version of the woven mat I decided to quilt a large crosshatch throughout the entire mat to add a bit of quilted feeling to the overall look. I stitched a diagonal line from every other corner to create the feel of traditional quilted crosshatching.

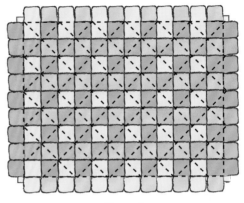

Step 4

Marigolds & Jam Placemats

Marigolds & Jam Placemats

Finished Dimensions: Four 15" × 21" placemats

I've always admired those beautiful quilted placemats at my favorite home stores. But somehow the colors or styles of them have never quite fit into our eclectic, fresh vintage look. When I started thinking of projects for the book, I immediately thought of making my own version of those much-admired placemats. The addition of the scallops makes them that much more special and seriously makes me want to sit down to a "proper breakfast" every day.

MATERIALS LIST

1 yard center fabric

1 yard border fabric

1 yard backing fabric

1 yard batting (or fusible fleece for the sewn version)

Freezer paper or tissue paper for pattern

Cutting Instructions for Sewn Placemats

For each placemat, cut the following:

- From the center fabric cut (1) 9½" × 15½" piece.
- From the border fabric cut (2) 3½" × 9½" pieces for the side borders.
- From the border fabric cut (2) 3½" × 21½" pieces for the top and bottom borders.
- From the backing fabric cut (1) 15½" × 12" piece and (1) 15½" × 11½" piece.
- From the fusible fleece cut (1) 15½" × 21½" piece.

Cutting Instructions for Quilted Placemats

For each placemat, cut the following:

- From the center fabric cut (1) 9½" × 15½" piece.
- From the border fabric cut (2) 3½" × 9½" pieces for the side borders.
- From the border fabric cut (2) 3½" × 21½" pieces for the top and bottom borders.
- From the backing fabric cut (1) 17" × 23" piece.
- From the backing fabric cut (2) 3⅞" × WOF facing pieces for the back.
- From the batting cut (1) 17" × 23" piece.

QUILTING TIP: If you plan on making more than one quilted placemat then I recommend quilting them together on one larger piece of backing fabric, all at the same time. Just lay out your backing and batting and position the placemat fronts on top. Pin and quilt them (see the quilting info on page 29).

Sewn Placemats Piecing Instructions

> **NOTE:** These placemats are made in the same way as the Saturday Morning Sham. Please refer to those additional diagrams when working through this pattern.

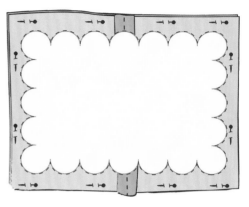

Step 5

1. Sew the side borders to the center. Press out. Sew the top and bottom borders to the center. Press out.
2. Line up the fusible fleece with the wrong side of the placemat and press. In order to prevent dimples in the fleece be sure to press well.
3. Turn under one short side of a backing piece ½" and press. Topstitch that fold down to create a finished fold. Repeat for the other short side. See Step 3 on pg. 104.
4. Line up the two back pieces on top of the placemat, folded sides in the center, RST. The pieces overlap slightly in the center and line up with the placemat along the edges. Pin well. See Step 4 on p. 105.
5. Using the larger of the two templates provided, press the template to the top. Center it and make sure that there is at least ¼" of seam allowance fabric all the way around the outer edges of the scallops. Sew along the outer line of the template all the way around. Be sure all your edges are still lined up as you sew. If you are working with tissue paper, pin to the fabric, trace the line, and proceed in the same manner. Sew carefully around each scallop and pivot at each inside point.
6. Peel off the paper and cut out the scallops with a ¼" seam allowance. Snip into the inner points, and cut out a bit of the seam allowance in each point. See Step 6 on p. 105.
7. Turn the backing sides RSO. Work each scallop one at a time. Start to work the fabric with your fingers and the iron to press nice crisp edges all the way around the scallops.
8. Press the placemat well, back and front. Pin the two back center folds together along the seam. Stitch the two backing pieces together by hand along the center.

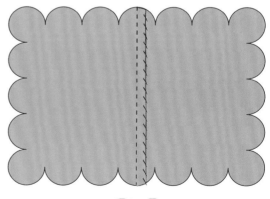

Step 8

9. Turn the placemat to the front and top-stitch all the way around the outside of the scallop, ¼" away from the edge. This step also helps the scallops retain a good shape after use.

Sew along the inside seam where the center and border join. Sew on the center side. Remove the pins. Repeat to make as many placemats as you need, and go make yourself that proper breakfast!

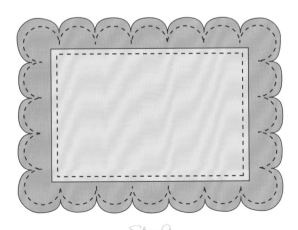

Step 9

Quilted Placemats Piecing Instructions

1. Repeat Step 1 from Sewn Placemat.
2. Create a quilt sandwich centering the placemat on the slightly bigger batting and backing. Pin together. Quilt as desired. I wanted mine to look like those favorites I had been admiring, so I chose to do similar quilting, crosshatching in the center portion and using a soft feathery swirl in the borders.
3. Roughly trim the excess batting and backing from around the placemat. Press the placemat well. Measure 3⅛" out from the inner seam of the border strips and trim the outer edges of your placemat to make it a rectangle, squaring up your placemat.

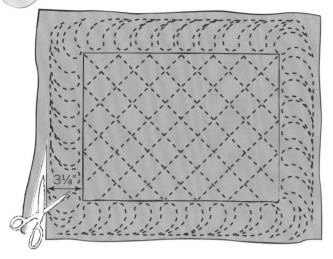

3⅛"

Step 3

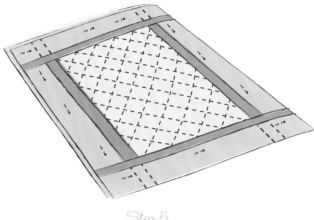

Step 5

QUILTING TIP: Use this "facing" method in order to get pretty scalloped borders and still see the quilting on the back of your placemat. The facing enables you to turn the scallops and the center of the placemat backing still shows the quilting instead of extra unnecessary fabric.

4. Measure the placemat and cut two facing pieces to the length and two pieces to the width measurement of your placemat. Fold one long side under ½" on each facing piece.

QUILTING TIP: Fabric will both shrink and distort during quilting so you might have slightly wobbly edges and a placemat that is smaller than what you started off with. If the measurement of your outer borders after quilting is smaller than 3⅛" then adjust that measurement accordingly. Don't be afraid to trim off any of the wobbly or distorted outer sides or corners.

5. Pin the side facing pieces to the front of the placemat, RST. Next, pin the top and bottom facing pieces to the placemat, RST. Try to keep the pins a bit toward the inside so that they don't interfere with the next step of sewing.

6. Using the smaller of the two templates provided, press the template to the top. Repeat Step 5 from the Sewn Version of the placemat. Be sure the edges of your quilt sandwich and the facing pieces are lined up along the outside as you sew. Sew carefully around each scallop and pivot at each inside point.

7. Repeat Step 6 from the Sewn Placemat.

8. Turn the facings RSO. Repeat Step 7 from the Sewn Placemat.

9. Press the placemat well, back and front. Pin the facings to the back of the placemat. Use a lot of pins in order to really secure these facings flat and in place. I emphasize this because the facings have

a tendency to move and wrinkle and tuck while you're sewing the next step.

shape after use. Last, sew along the inside seam where the center and border join. Sew on the center side. This should just catch the seam on the finished edge of the facings all the way around. Remove the pins. Repeat to make as many placemats as you need and invite a friend or two to that proper breakfast!

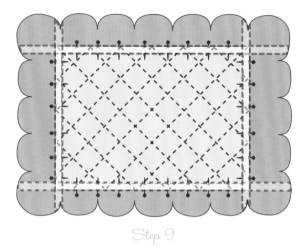

Step 9

10. Turn the placemat to the front and top-stitch all the way around the outside of the scallop, ¼" away from the edge. This step also helps the scallops retain a good

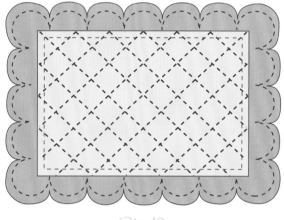

Step 10

Chapter 7

Quilting Projects

Whereas the projects in the other chapters span the gamut of sewing and quilting accessories and clothing, this chapter is purely about my first love. The quilts I chose are shown to you in variations and different color options because I want you to see how fabric placement can drastically change the final outcome of your project. You can create contemporary or classic results simply through the fabric you use. I love that about fabric. The projects I have chosen here also span the spectrum from large blocks to mini ones, from pieced work to a bit of appliqué. I hope you enjoy every single one of these projects and that they warm and decorate your home for decades to come.

Slipper Booties

Slipper Booties

Snuggling Up In Style

Finished Dimensions: Little Kid's Sizes 6-12 and Big Kid's Sizes 13-6

One of our all-time best-selling patterns is one I designed many years ago for children's slippers. These booties are simple and easily customizable, and they have always been a hit. What I was going for here was the next generation of slippers; these little booties are literally that—slippers that easily turn into the sweetest boots for the little feet in your life. The pattern works great for both girls and boys up to whatever size they are still willing to wear them! I have made them for my younger two children, but I guarantee that when winter rolls around, the 13-year-old will be asking for a pair of his own, although he might request a cooler fabric.

NOTE: Customize your booties by using a coordinating fabric on the inside. Remember that the inside fabric shows when you cuff the booties.

MATERIALS LIST

⅜ to ½ yard slipper exterior fabric (⅜ yard for the smaller sizes; ½ yard for the larger)

⅜ to ½ yard slipper interior fabric (⅜ for the smaller sizes; ½ yard for the larger)

⅜ to ½ yard batting (⅜ for the smaller sizes; ½ yard for the larger)

¼ yard coordinating binding fabric

Cutting Instructions

NOTE: Before you begin cutting, you need to quilt the fabric as described in Step 1 of the "Assembly Instructions."

- From the slipper fabric cut (2) templates of the slipper top (choose appropriate template size).
- From the slipper fabric cut (2) templates of the boot (choose appropriate template size).
- From the slipper fabric cut (2) templates of the slipper sole/bottom (choose appropriate template size).
- From the binding fabric cut (1) 2¼" × WOF strip of binding and then cut it into (2) 16" lengths for kid sizes and up to 20" for the larger sizes depending on the width of the shoe top. Check your slipper size to make sure you are cutting enough length to go around the top of both your slippers plus 12" extra for finishing off. Cut your strip in half so you have one piece for each slipper.
- From the interior fabric cut (1) 2¼" × WOF strip of binding and then cut it into (2) 10" pieces for the small kid sizes and at least 12" for the larger sizes. Check the length of the back of your slipper to make sure you are cutting enough length to span the entire back of the slipper.

Assembly Instructions

1. Make a quilt sandwich with the slipper exterior fabric, the batting, and the slipper interior fabric, which in this case is also the back of your quilt sandwich. Quilt as desired. I quilted a simple all-over design.

2. From the quilted fabric, cut the pieces described in the "Cutting Instructions."

3. Find the center of the boot piece and the center of the slipper top piece and pin in place, RST. Pin in both directions from this center point to each edge and secure the two pieces together. Sew the boot piece to the slipper top piece. Remove the pins. Finish the remaining seam with a zigzag stitch or another favorite finishing stitch. Going forward I refer to this piece as the "slipper top piece".

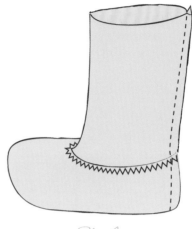

Step 4

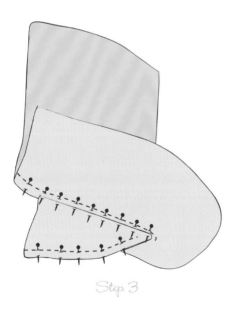

Step 3

4. Fold the slipper top piece in half, RST and pin the back raw edges together. Sew it shut along the back seam.

5. Because the top of this section shows when you cuff the slipper top, you need to cover the slipper back seam with a single-fold binding of sorts. To do this, fold one long side of the interior fabric binding strip under ½". Lay the remaining raw binding side along the back sewn seam, lining up all the raw edges together. Sew the edge of the single fold binding piece to the slipper top with a ¼" seam.

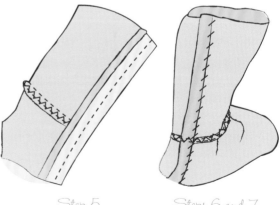

Step 5   Steps 6 and 7

6. Turn the folded side of the binding over and lay it flat along the slipper, pulling the slipper raw edges flat with it as you pull. Pin.

7. Stitch the binding to the slipper by hand to create a nicely enclosed and flat back seam.

8. Place the slipper top piece on the sole/bottom slipper piece, RST. Pin the two pieces together starting with a pin on the middle of the toe and another pin on the back seam. Ease the rest of the slipper top onto the bottom, pinning all the way around. Sew all the way around. Finish the remaining seams with a zigzag stitch or another favorite finishing stitch. Remove the pins and flip the slipper RSO. Push the shape out with your fingers.

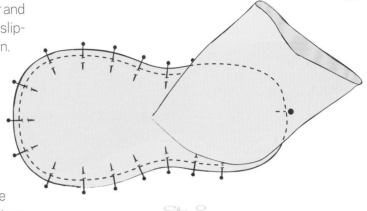

Step 8

9. Repeat Steps 3 to 8 for the second slipper.

10. Finish off the top of the slipper with another piece of single-fold binding. Fold and press under ¼" of one long side of your binding piece and pin the other side to the slipper and sew in place. Follow the single fold binding directions in Chapter 2 to finish the binding.

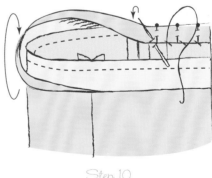

Step 10

11. Cuff the slipper if you like or keep as boot and enjoy!

Summer Soiree Patchwork Quilt

Summer Soiree Patchwork Quilt

Picnicking in Style

Finished Dimensions: 52" × 65" ▪ (20) 13" Blocks

One of my favorite parts of the quilting process is choosing fabrics to create those yummy little fabric stacks that makes quilters dream. I know this is going to sound funny, but, as a fabric designer, I don't get many opportunities to play with whatever fabric strikes my fancy because I am usually working to showcase one particular new fabric collection. When I'm working on a book, however, I can play with fabrics to my heart's content!

Even though my prints are usually considered to be on the more traditional side of the spectrum, my colors are often vibrant and fresh, and I love working with that mix of vintage and new as often as I can.

In these projects, mixing my own fabrics with classic modern designs like those of Kaffe Fassett and Amy Butler was like playing with a box of watercolors—all the colors blended seamlessly from one to another. I know that most people would not think to use such different styles of fabric together, but because the palette is the same, I think you might agree that the result is just good enough to eat!

NOTE: In case you would like to make both the Summer Soiree and Tagalong Sister quilts as companion projects, please reference the Tagalong Sister Materials List Note before purchasing fabrics.

MATERIALS LIST

14 various ¼ yards in peach/apricot, apple green, aqua, lavender, tangerine, sky blue, caramel, cream, coral (backgrounds)

1¼ yard cream solid or small cream print for the appliqué (such as the small cream dot I used)

1¼ yard cream muslin or other cream solid foundation fabric that matches your appliqué fabric

3¼ yards backing

½ yard solid coral (binding)

Freezer paper

Cutting Instructions

- From (14) various colors cut (1) 7" × WOF strip. Cut each strip into (6) 7" squares. You need a total of (80) squares.
- From the cream print cut (14) 3" × WOF strips. Cut into (80) 3" × 7" rectangles. Create a freezer paper template and trace a leaf shape onto the wrong side of each one.
- From the cream muslin cut (14) 3" × WOF strips. Cut into (80) 3 × 7" rectangles.
- From the coral solid cut (7) 2¼" binding strips.

Piecing Instructions

1. Sew the 7" squares into "light/dark" pairs. Press toward the "dark" side. Match two pairs with alternating lights and darks and sew the pairs into 4-patches. Sew (20) 4-patches.

> **DESIGN TIP:** The reason I chose this appliqué method is that these appliqué leaves are a single layer and the bright colors underneath would show right through. This method yields double fabric appliqué shapes and has a great result when using a light fabric appliqué on top of bright fabrics.

2. Using a design wall or a large floor space, lay out all of the 4-patches, four across and five down as shown until you like the way the colors lay out across the entire quilt top. Sew the 4-patches into five rows of four 4-patches each. Press row #1 to the left, row #2 to the right, row #3 to the left and so forth. Alternating the pressing is important so that the rows interlock when you add them to one another.

3. Prepare the appliqué pieces by laying a cream print rectangle RST with a cream muslin background rectangle. Sew the pairs together on the drawn line, all the way around. Cut the shape out, adding a ¼" seam allowance all the way around the drawn sew line. Trim a bit closer than a ¼" on the tips to eliminate some of the excess fabric. Cut a center slit approximately 2" in the cream muslin background

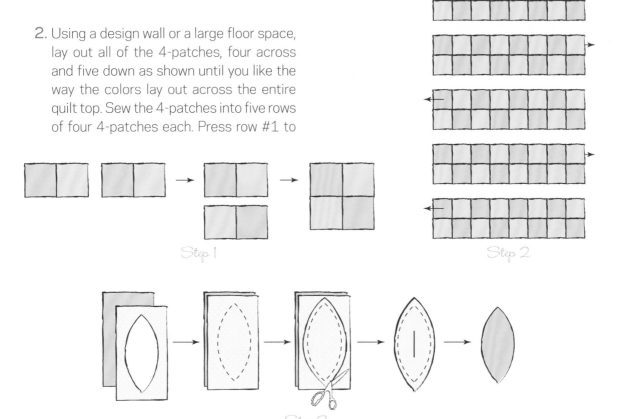

Step 1

Step 2

Step 3

and turn the fabric RSO. Press the leaf well, all the way around.

4. Position the leaf templates on each row as shown. Glue or pin in place and machine appliqué the leaves down on each row. Repeat for all five rows.

5. Sew the five rows together. Press the entire quilt top well.

Step 4

QUILTING HINT: Usually in quilting when you are using light and dark fabrics, there is a strong difference between the colors and the lights and darks are very easily distinguishable. In this case, the differences are slight and not that important. Try to roughly divide the pairs into "lighter" and "darker" in order to maintain visual interest but don't worry too much about these fabric combinations.

QUILTING HINT: Pressing a shape well all the way around takes a lot of patience and at least a little bit of practice. To get the best shape, I recommend pushing the edges and especially the corners out with some kind of a long blunt object. Fancy chopsticks are perfect for the job as are presser bars, that you can purchase for this step.

Step 5

6. Make a quilt sandwich and quilt as desired. I chose to outline-stitch the leaf appliqué shapes and stitch a small all-over feather design throughout the background blocks in order to blend the entire background and help to pop the appliqué design.

7. Bind using (7) 2¼" binding strips.

Tagalong Sister Quilt

Something of Their Own

Finished Dimensions: 43" × 55" ▪ (12) 12" Blocks

As I worked on the Summer Soiree project, I realized that I had all kinds of wonderful, colorful leftovers that I couldn't bear to part with. Instead of going into my standard leftover pile, I created a scrap or "tagalong" project from everything I had left.

Our own family picnic trips seem to always end up with too many goodies and not enough space for all the very energetic kids! So the next time around, the kids will have their own picnic with their own goodies, and they'll be able enjoy it on their very own picnic quilt. A sister version to Summer Soiree, this quilt can be done with these project leftovers or any grouping of colorful scraps from your stash.

NOTE: If you want to make both of these projects then you need (16) 3/8 yards total of all the various colors mentioned in the Summer Soiree description. Simply add the necessary cream, muslin, backing, and binding yardage for both quilts.

MATERIALS LIST

(16) ⅛ yards of the same colors as used in Summer Soiree

1¾ yards cream print for the appliqué and border (I used the same cream dot here as I used in the Summer Soiree quilt)

1⅛ yard cream muslin (appliqué backing)

2¾ yards backing

½ yard binding

Freezer paper

Cutting Instructions

- From the (16) ⅛ yards cut (1) 3 ½" × WOF strip from *each* color. Cut each strip into (12) 3½" squares. You need a total of (192) 3½" squares.
- From the cream print cut (12) 3" × WOF strips. Cut them into (48) 3" × 9" rectangles. Create a freezer paper template and trace a leaf template shape onto the wrong side of each rectangle.
- From the cream print cut (5) 4" × WOF strips. Cut (2) strips into (2) 4" × 36½" top and bottom borders. Piece the remaining (3) strips for length and cut them into (2) 4" × 55½" left- and right-side borders.
- From the cream muslin or solid cut (12) 3" × WOF strips. Cut them into (48) 3" × 9" rectangles.
- From binding fabric cut (6) 2¼" binding strips.

Piecing Instructions

1. Sew the 3½" squares into "light/dark" pairs. Press toward the "dark" side. Match two pairs with alternating lights and darks and sew the pairs into 4-patches. Sew (48) 4-patches. See Summer Soiree for more info (p.150).

2. Using a design wall or a large floor space, lay out all of the 4-patches six across and eight down as shown until you like the way the colors lay out across the entire quilt top. Sew the 4-patches into eight rows of six 4-patches each. Press row #1 to the left, row #2 to the right, row #3 to the left, and so on, alternating the pressing direction for the rest of the rows. Alternating the pressing is important so that the rows interlock when you add them to one another.

3. Join the rows into pairs so that you have four rows of (12) 4-patches.

4. Prepare the appliqué pieces in the same way as in Summer Soiree (p. 150).

5. Position the leaf templates on each double row as shown. Note that the leaf shape is larger and the placement is different

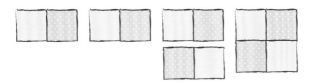

Step 1

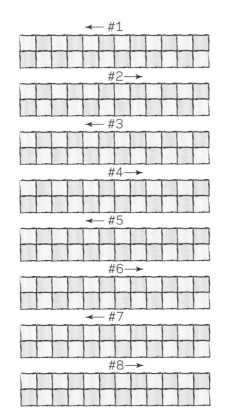

Step 2

Step 5

than in the Summer Soiree project. Glue or pin the leaves in place and machine appliqué them down on each row.

6. Sew the four double rows together. Press the entire quilt top well.

7. Add the top and bottom borders first. Press out. Add the left and right borders second. Press out.

8. Make a quilt sandwich and quilt as desired. I chose to outline-stitch the leaf appliqué shapes and stitch a small all-over feather design throughout the background blocks in order to blend the entire background and help to pop the design.

9. Bind using (6) 2¼" binding strips.

Strawberries and Cream Table Runner

Strawberries and Cream Table Runner

Finished Size: 19½" × 59½" ▪ (17) 5" Basket Blocks

As long as I have been designing quilts, I have been in love with basket quilts. In fact, I am not sure that I have ever seen a basket quilt, especially a vintage one, that I did not admire. It is just such a classic and simple block to make, and it has such a wonderful effect and shape. When I was working out a table runner design, I focused on what I would want on our table, which is a very long farm table made from recycled floor planks from a British pub. I knew I wanted something creamy and soft with punches of color that would fit on the table for most of the seasons of the year. The scrappy cream background with all floral baskets came to life, and I fell in love with it right away. You might remember me talking about cutting up florals in the color chapter, and this is a great example of that technique. Each basket feels different and unique even though only a few fabrics are used.

MATERIALS LIST

(6) ¼ yard various large floral prints for baskets

(8) ⅛ yard cream prints for 4-patches

(2) ¼ yard cream solid or tone on tone for basket background (You can also use just one fabric here. I used two different creams for a bit of extra variety.)

⅜" bias tape maker (to make the handles)

½ yard outer border

1⅓ yards backing

⅜ yard binding

Basting glue

Cutting Instructions

- From *each* color floral fabric cut (3) ¾" bias strips from the end of your yardage before you begin cutting the rest of the pieces.
- From *each* color floral fabric cut (2) 4⅞" squares. Cut in half on the diagonal for a total of (4) triangles [a]. You need 3 out of the 4 of each floral fabric for a total of (17) triangles.
- From *each* color floral fabric cut (3) 1⅞" squares. Cut in half on the diagonal for a total of (6) triangles [b]. Need 6 of each. Need (34) triangles total.
- From *each* of the various background cream fabrics cut (1) 3" × WOF strip. Cut into (8) 3" squares [c]. Need (64) squares total.
- From *each* of the various background cream fabrics cut (2) 1½" × WOF strips. Cut into (18) 1½" × 3½" pieces [d]. Need (34) pieces total.

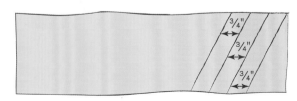

Bias strip cutting diagram

- From *each* of the various background cream fabrics cut (1) 4⅞" × WOF strip. Cut into (5) 4⅞" squares. Cut in half on the diagonal for a total of (10) triangles [e] from each fabric. Need (17) triangles total.
- From the leftovers of the cream 4⅞" strip cut (5) 2⅞" squares. Cut in half on the diagonal for a total of (10) triangles [f] from each fabric. Need 17 triangles total.

> **NOTE:** You are cutting a few pieces extra in several of the cutting instructions here. This is because you are cutting from several different backgrounds and it also gives you a few more choices when making combinations as you sew. I recommend making little piles of cream pieces (that is, one large triangle, two rectangles, etc.) that you need for each basket as you cut. Do this with the color florals as well. Then when it comes time to start constructing blocks, simply add a floral "pile" to one of the cream "piles" and you are ready to go.

- From the border fabric cut (5) 2¾" × WOF strips. Piece for length and cut (2)

2¾" × 60" left- and right-side borders and (2) 2¾" × 24½" top and bottom borders.
- From the binding fabric cut (5) 2¼" binding strips.

Piecing Instructions

1. Run the ¾" bias strips through a ⅜" bias tape maker to make a finished piece of bias tape.
2. Cut out the basket guideline template from freezer paper. Press it to the center of a 4⅞" background triangle [e]. Place small dots of basting glue around the outside of the paper template. Place the bias tape along the template, pressing down to affix with the glue. Press gently in place.
3. Trim the ends of the bias tape, extending them approximately ¼" beyond the end of the triangle on each end. Peel off the paper template. Appliqué the handle to the background by hand or by machine.
4. Sew a color triangle [b] to the end of each background rectangle [d]. Press toward the

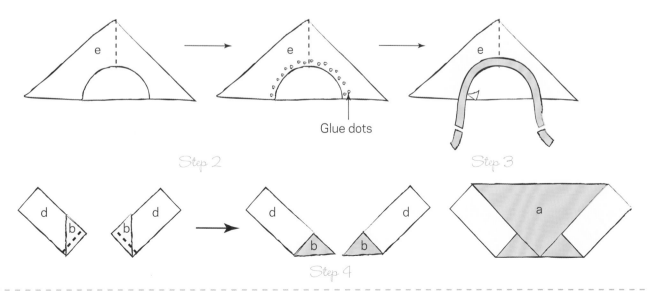

Glue dots

Step 2   Step 3

Step 4

triangle. Be sure to note the placement of the triangle on the diagram as each of the two triangles is facing the opposite direction. Sew each unit to the side of the color triangle [a]. Press toward the color triangle [a] after sewing on each side.

5. Sew the background triangle [f] to the bottom of the block. Press out toward the background triangle [f].

> **NOTE:** Be sure that you sew on the side of the basket triangles so that as you sew you can see the bottom point of the basket and "catch it" in your seam. This is one of those little quilting tricks to make sure that you catch your point as you sew. You always have a chance to veer a tiny bit in or out if you are a little off.

6. Add the handle section to the top of the basket section. Press toward the basket.

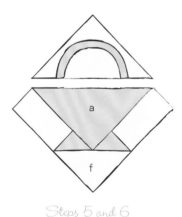

Steps 5 and 6

7. Sew the squares [c] into pairs. Press in one direction. Flip one pair over and sew pairs into 4-patches. Press in one direction. Make a total of (16) 4-patch blocks.

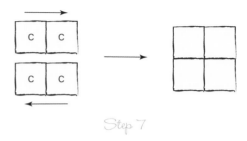

Step 7

Assembly Instructions

1. Assemble the basket blocks and the 4-patch blocks into rows of three, alternating the blocks as shown in the diagram. Press toward the 4-patch blocks each time. Repeat to make (11) rows, (6) that start and end with a basket block and (5) that start and end with a 4-patch block. Note the direction of the basket blocks in each type of rows as they alternate directions.

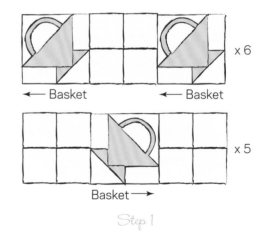

Step 1

2. Add the rows to one another, always pressing the seams to the same side. Alternate the two kinds of rows as you sew, taking care to sew them in the correct direction.

3. Add the side borders to the left and right sides. Press out. Add the top and bottom borders to the top and bottom. Press out.

4. Make a quilt sandwich and quilt as desired. Diana quilted tiny ¾" crosshatches on all of the baskets to resemble woven basket work. She outlined the handles and added a little half flower in the handle space. She filled in the background with a small all-over feather design and added a simple feather to the border.

5. Bind using (5) 2¼" binding strips.

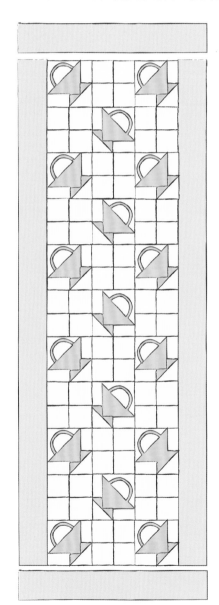

Blossom Quilt: Meadow Version

Blossom Quilt

Meadow, Maison, and Cherry Blossoms

Finished Dimensions: 75" × 75" ▪ (9) 20" Blocks

Because I am a quilter at heart, I love working on patchwork quilts with lots of pieces and as many different fabrics as possible. But once in a while I want to work on something big, simple, and graphic. When I designed this block, I instantly fell in love with the "blossom" feel of it and the simplicity with which it came together. I am always amazed at how you can make simple pieced blocks look like they have curves and complexity! I designed this quilt in at least a dozen variations and chose these two sizes in three colorways as my favorites to share with you. I love the spring green version for its striking and modern simplicity. I love the taupe gray and cream version for its French country feel and sophistication. This is probably the one that I will use and love the most! I love the red and cream version for its simple, classic feel in one of my all-time favorite color combinations!

Meadow Blossom or Maison Blossom

Cutting Instructions

If using all one cream solid fabric as in Meadow Blossom:
- Cut (12) 5½" × WOF cream strips. Cut them into (81) 5½" squares [d].

or

If using (9) different cream prints as in Maison Blossom:
- Cut (2) 5½" × WOF strips from *each* of (9) different cream fabrics. Cut into (9) 5½" squares [d] from *each* cream fabric print so you have a total of (81) 5½" cream squares [d].

For either version
- From solid or extra accent cream: cut (8) 1½" × WOF cream accent border strips. Piece for length and cut into (2) 1½" × 66½" left and right accent borders and (2) 1½" × 68½" top and bottom accent borders.
- From green or taupe gray background fabric, cut (32) 3" × WOF strips. Cut (16) 3" × WOF strips into (216) 3" squares [a]. Cut (16) 3" strips into (108) 3" × 5½" pieces [b].

MATERIALS LIST

2½ yards cream solid *or* (9) ⅜ yards various cream prints (blossom blocks)

4¾ yards green or taupe gray (background)

½ yard extra cream (accent border—only for Maison Blossom version)

4½ yards backing

⅝ yards green or taupe gray (binding)

- From green or taupe gray background fabric, cut (2) 1¾" × WOF strips. Cut into (36) 1¾" squares [c].
- From green or taupe gray background fabric, cut (6) 2½" × WOF strips. Cut into (6) 2½" × 20½" sashings [e]. Piece the (3) remaining strips together for length. Cut into (2) 2½" × 64½" sashing strips [f].
- From green or taupe gray background fabric, cut (8) 1½" × WOF inner border strips. Piece for length and cut into (2) 1½" × 64½" left and right inner borders and (2) 1½" × 66½" top and bottom inner borders.
- From green or taupe gray background fabric, cut (8) 4" × WOF outer border strips. Piece for length and cut into (2) 4" × 68½" left and right outer borders and (2) 4" × 75½" top and bottom outer borders.

Piecing Instructions

1. Sew a background square [c] on the diagonal to the four corners of a cream square [d] following the method explained in the "Basics" section on page 25. This is your center unit [A].

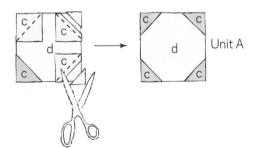

Step 1

(diagram labels) Unit A

Step 2   Step 3

Unit B

2. Sew a background square [a] on the diagonal to only two corners of a cream square [d] following the same method on page 25. Repeat to make four units [B].
3. Add a background piece [b] to the side of each unit [B]. Press outward toward [b].
4. Sew a background square [a] on the diagonal to three corners of a cream square [d] following the same method on page 25. Repeat to make four units [C].
5. Sew a background piece [b] to the right side of each unit [C]. Press outward toward [b].

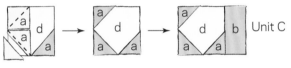

Steps 4 and 5

Unit C

6. Sew a background square [a] to one end of a background piece [b]. Press toward the piece [b]. Repeat to make four units.

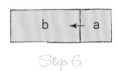

Step 6

7. Sew the piece you created in Step 6 to the top of each unit [C] as shown. Press outward.

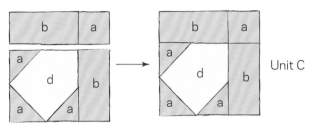

Unit C

Step 7

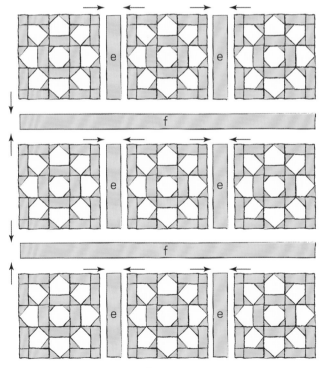

Step 8: Finished Block

8. Using one unit [A], four units [B], and four units [C], assemble the units into three rows. Note the differing placement of the units as you go around the block. Add the rows together to create the block according to the diagram. Be sure to press toward unit [B] each time. Repeat to make nine blocks. Your blocks should measure 20½" with seam allowance.

9. Using the blocks and sashing pieces [e], assemble the blocks into three rows of three as shown. Press toward the sashing each time.

10. Add the three rows together by alternating block rows with sashing strips [f] as shown. Press toward the sashings. Press the quilt center well.

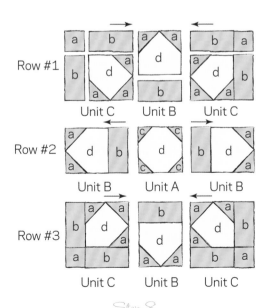

Step 8

Steps 9 and 10

11. Add the left and right side of the inner border. Press toward the border. Add the top and bottom inner border. Press toward the border.

12. Add the left and right side of the middle accent border. Press toward the accent border. Add the top and bottom middle accent border. Press toward the accent border.

13. Add the left and right side of the outer border. Press toward the outer border. Add the top and bottom outer border. Press toward the outer border.

14. Make a quilt sandwich and quilt as desired. For the Meadow version, Diana quilted a large clamshell design over the entire green and cream patchwork for a more contemporary look. For the Maison version, she cross-hatched the centers, created a wreath in each blossom, and quilted a small all-over feather design in the rest of the quilt.

15. Bind using (8) 2¼" binding strips.

Blossom Quilt: Maison Version

Cherry Blossom Quilt

Cherry Blossom

Finished Dimensions: 66" × 66" ▪ (9) 16" Blocks

One of the wonderful things about designing several patterns with the same design is that you get to see how color placement and quilting can completely alter the end product. In this case, a slightly smaller block, the addition of a few corners and posts, and a traditional color scheme creates a completely different quilt. A classic design that is perfect for every day and for the holidays as well.

DESIGN TIP: The construction itself on both styles of this quilt is identical. The small difference, other than size, is that the Cherry Blossom blocks have a different color in the corners whereas the Meadow and Maison Blossom blocks simply have the same color as their background fabric in that position. The Cherry Blossom version also has red posts added into the sashings, whereas the other two versions have a single color background. Study these quilts and think about which look and feel you prefer and go from there.

MATERIALS LIST

(9) ¼ yards in various red print fabrics (blossom blocks)

3⅞ yards solid cream (background)

¼ yard small gray print (block corners)

4 yards backing

½ yard solid red (binding)

Cutting Instructions

- From each of (9) red block fabrics cut (1) 4½" × WOF strip. Cut it into (9) 4½" squares [d].
- From the cream background fabric cut (11) 2½" × WOF strips. Cut into (180) 2½" squares [a].
- From the cream background fabric cut (12) 2½" × WOF strips. Cut into (108) 2½" × 4½" pieces [b].
- From the cream background fabric cut (2) 1½" × WOF strips. Cut into (36) 1½" squares [c].
- From the cream background fabric cut (12) 2½" × WOF strips. Cut into (24) 2½" × 16½" sashings [e].
- From the cream background fabric cut (6) 2½" × WOF strips. Piece for length and cut into (4) 2½" × 56½" border strips [f].
- From the cream background fabric cut (7) 3½" × WOF outer border strips. Piece for length and cut into (2) 3½" × 60½" left and right outer borders and (2) 3½" × 66½" top and bottom outer borders.
- From the gray fabric for the block corners cut (3) 2½" × WOF strips. Cut into (40) 2½" squares [g].
- From the leftovers of one of the small red prints cut (1) 2½" × WOF strip. Cut into (16) 2½" squares [h] for posts.
- From the solid red print cut (7) 2¼" × WOF binding strips.

Piecing Instructions

1. Follow Steps 1–5 as in the Meadow and Maison Blossom instructions.

> **QUILTING NOTE:** Remember the "Breaking My Own Rule" exception on page 26? It applies here. In the case of both the Meadow and Maison Blossom quilts, I recommend keeping all the pieces intact and not cutting out any of the excess corner fabric. The pieces are nice and big here and the bulk does not hurt the design in this case.

2. Sew a gray square [g] to one side of a background rectangle [b]. Press toward the rectangle. Repeat four times.

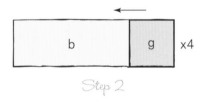

Step 2

3. Sew the piece you created in Step 2 to the side of each unit [C] as shown. Press outward.

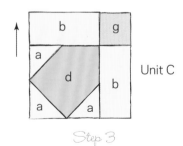

Step 3

4. Using one unit [A], four units [B], and four units [C], assemble the block according to the diagram. Be sure to press rows according to the arrows. Repeat to make nine blocks.

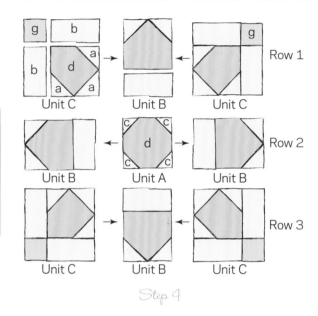

Unit C | Unit B | Unit C — Row 1
Unit B | Unit A | Unit B — Row 2
Unit C | Unit B | Unit C — Row 3

Step 4

5. Using three blocks and two sashing pieces [e] for each row, assemble the blocks into three rows of three as shown. Press toward the sashing each time.

6. Create six sashing rows by alternating three sashings [e] with two red post squares [h] for each row. Always press toward the sashing pieces.

7. Sew the block rows together by alternating them with four of the sashing rows. Start and end with a sashing row as shown. Press toward the sashing rows.

8. Sew a red post square [h] to each end of the two remaining sashing rows. Press toward the sashing. Add those sashing rows to the left and right sides of the quilt. Press outward.

9. Sew a [f] cream border to the left and right side of the quilt. Press outward.

10. Add gray corner squares [g] to both ends of the two remaining [f] cream borders. Sew them to the top and bottom of the quilt. Press outward.

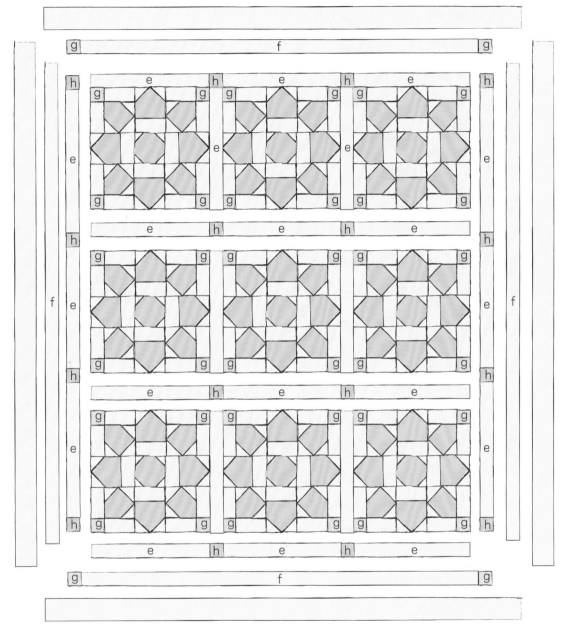

Steps 5-11

11. Sew the 3½" × 60½" outer cream borders to the sides. Press outward. Sew the 3½" × 66½" outer cream borders to the top and bottom. Press outward.

12. Make a quilt sandwich and quilt as desired. Diana cross-hatched the centers, created a feather wreath in each blossom, stippled the background and added a feather border.

13. Bind using (8) 2¼" binding strips.

Fresh Vintage Patchwork

Finished Measurements: 62" × 77" ▪ (30) 6" Blocks

As I set to work on what quilts I thought had to be a part of this book, my mind immediately went to the traditional house block. Probably the most iconic of all classic quilt blocks, the house block has not only been around for centuries in every imaginable folk art, but it is also possibly my favorite quilt block. (Not to mention that the first book I ever worked on, many years ago, was one with all house quilts in it.) As you can imagine, the house block holds a special place near and dear to my heart. This version is a classic Fig Tree-style quilt with a combination background of creams mixed in with some of these wonderful "forgotten" colors.

NOTE: To make things simpler, all instructions are given assuming that you are making the 9-patch blocks throughout the quilt. If you are adding the house block, you will have a few extra blocks.

MATERIALS LIST

(7) ¼ yards various color prints (taupes, greens, butterscotch, gray, olive, charcoal, coral, chocolate, pumpkin) for the blocks

(7) ⅓ yards various cream prints for the backgrounds

1½ yard solid cream for sashing

1 yard for outer border

3¾ yards backing

⅝ yard for binding

(6) ⅛ yards for the house (yellow=house, green=house bottom, butterscotch=door, grey=windows, red=roof, olive=chimneys)

Cutting Instructions

- From *each* of (7) color prints cut (3) 2" × WOF strips. Cut all the strips in half crosswise. Reserve (4) of the half-strips for unit construction. Cut (8) 2" corner post squares [a] from the fifth half-strip. Need (52) total. Set the sixth half-strip aside completely for another project.
- From *each* of (7) background cream prints cut (1) 6½" × WOF strip. Cut into (5) 6½" cream alternate squares [b]. Need (31) total.
- From *each* of (7) background cream prints cut (1) 3½" × WOF strip. Cut in half crosswise. Reserve (1) of the half-strips for unit construction. Cut (10) 3½" × 2" pieces [c] from the remaining half-strip. Need (64) total.
- From the cream solid sashing cut (19) 2" × WOF strips. Cut each strip into (6) 2" × 6½" sashings [d]. Need (110) total.

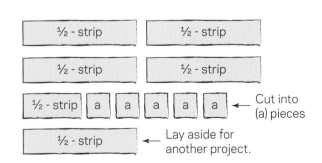

- From the cream solid sashing cut (6) 2" × WOF strips. Piece for length into 2 pairs of 3-strips each. From *each* sewn set of 3-strips cut (1) 2" × 66½" left/right inner border and (1) 2" × 51½" top/bottom inner border.

For House block:
- Cut (10) 1¾" × 2½" for windows [e].
- Cut (1) 3" × 4" for door [f].
- Cut (1) 3½" × 14" for roof [g].
- Cut (2) 1¾" × 2¼" for chimneys [h].
- Cut (1) 2" × 14" for house bottom [i].
- Cut (2) 3½" squares [j], (2) 2¼" × 3½" [k], and (1) 2¼" × 5½" [m] for background.
- Cut (10) 1¼" × 2½" [n]; (3) 2" × 2½" [o]; (2) 2" × 6" [p]; (1) 1¼" × 14" [q]; (1) 1½" × 14" [r] for the house.
- Cut (2) 2" × WOF strips. Cut into (2) 2" × 14" side sashing pieces [s] and (2) 2" × 17" top/bottom sashing pieces [t].
- From outer border cut (7) 4½" × WOF strips. Piece for length and cut into (2) 4½" × 69½" left and right borders and (2) 4½" × 62½" top and bottom borders.
- From binding cut (8) 2¼" × WOF strips.

Piecing Instructions

1. For each of the four half-strips of each color, organize as follows:
   a. Take two half-strips of color #1 and match with one cream half-strip for the pieces for Unit 1.
   b. Take one half-strip of color #1 and match with a color #2/accent halfstrip for the pieces for Unit 2.

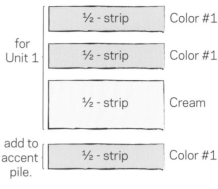

Step 1: Unit 1

c. Take the ten cream pieces [c] from the same cream print used above and place with the above strips for Unit 2.
d. Take the last half-strip of color #1 and place it in a separate pile. You will choose from this pile when you need the color #2/accent strip for any of the other fabric combo sets you are making. Basically this color #1 strip will become your color #2/accent strip in another combo. (This will all make more sense when you start making groupings than it probably does now!)

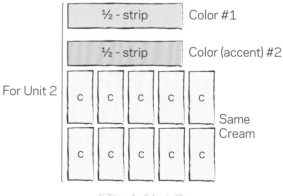

Step 1: Unit 2

Repeat this process of matching and creating groupings with all seven colors and all seven creams, using three half-strips of one main color, a fourth half-strip of an accent color as well as one cream background half-strip and the ten matching cream [c] pieces.

When finished you will have seven fabric groupings that make up all the pieces you need for each set of blocks. You will be making five blocks from each.

> **NOTE:** The following instructions are for sewing five blocks at a time from each grouping from Step 1.

2. To make Unit 1, sew a color #1 half-strip to the top and bottom of the cream half-strip. Press in toward the cream strip. Cut into (10) 2" × 6½" Units 1.

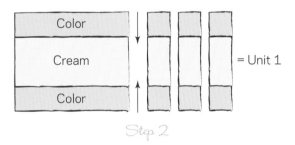

Step 2

3. To make Unit 2, sew a color #1 half-strip to the accent color half-strip. Press to one side. Cut the strip set into (10) 2" × 3½" 2-patch pairs. Turn one of the 2-patch pairs around and sew them into pairs. Press to one side. Make (5) 4-patches.

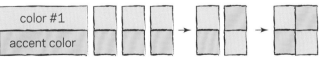

Step 3

4. Add a cream [c] piece to the top and bottom of the 4-patch you created in Step 3. Press toward the cream [c] piece each time. Complete five Units 2.

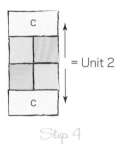

Step 4

5. To complete the patchwork block, sew a Unit 1 to each side of a Unit 2. Press out toward Unit 1 each time. Complete the five patchwork blocks from this grouping.

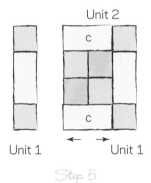

Step 5

6. Repeat with the remaining six groupings to make a total of (32) patchwork blocks. Note that if you are making the house block, you only need to make (30) patchwork blocks.

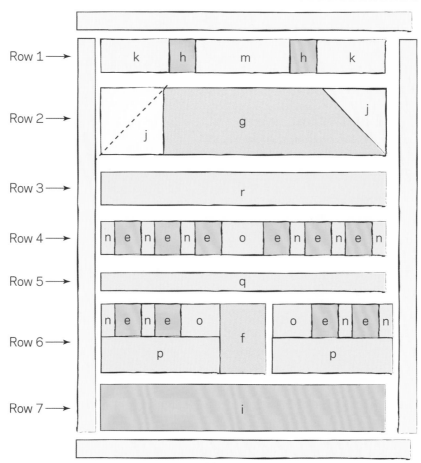

Row 1 →

Row 2 →

Row 3 →

Row 4 →

Row 5 →

Row 6 →

Row 7 →

House diagram

Assembly Instructions

NOTE: If you are adding the house block, assemble the quilt top by starting with house block rows 6 and 7. Sew the patchwork blocks into pairs with the alternate cream squares [b], sashing with (3) solid cream [d]. Press toward the sashing [d] each time. Join the block pairs together by alternating with "a-d-a-d-a" sashings as shown. Add the house block in place of two of the standard block pairs. Finish the section and piece this 2-row section into the rest of the quilt using the following directions.

NOTE: Please remember that with this house block addition you will have fewer rows to construct: four block rows that start with a patchwork block, three block rows that start with a cream alternate square, and five sashing rows.

1. Begin to assemble the *block rows* as shown in the diagrams, alternating patchwork blocks with alternate cream squares [b] and sashing with (6) solid cream [d]. Press toward the sashing [d] each time. Sew five rows that begin and end with a patchwork block. Sew four rows that begin and end with an alternate cream square [b].

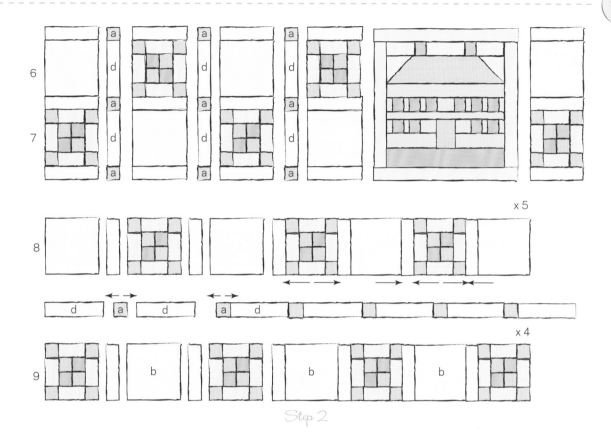

Step 2

2. Assemble (8) *sashing rows* by sewing (7) solid cream sashings [d] and (6) square posts [a] together as shown. Press toward the sashing [d] each time.

3. Alternate the block rows and sashing rows as shown, starting and ending with a row that begins with a patchwork block. Press toward the sashing rows each time.

4. Sew the inner cream solid borders to the left and right sides. Press out toward the inner border.

5. Sew a corner post square [a] to each end of the top and bottom inner borders. Press toward the borders. Sew the inner borders to the top and bottom. Press out toward the inner borders.

6. Sew the left and right outer borders. Press out. Sew the top and bottom outer borders. Press out.

7. Make a quilt sandwich and quilt as desired. Diana chose to do a square version of a wreath block in each cream alternate space and stipple the inside of each wreath. She quilted a straight line through the entire chain throughout the quilt and finished off the outer border with scalloped half wreaths. She did some decorative quilting on the house including scalloped tiles on the roof, X's through the windows and doors and an outline around the rest of the house.

8. Bind, using (8) 2¼" binding strips.

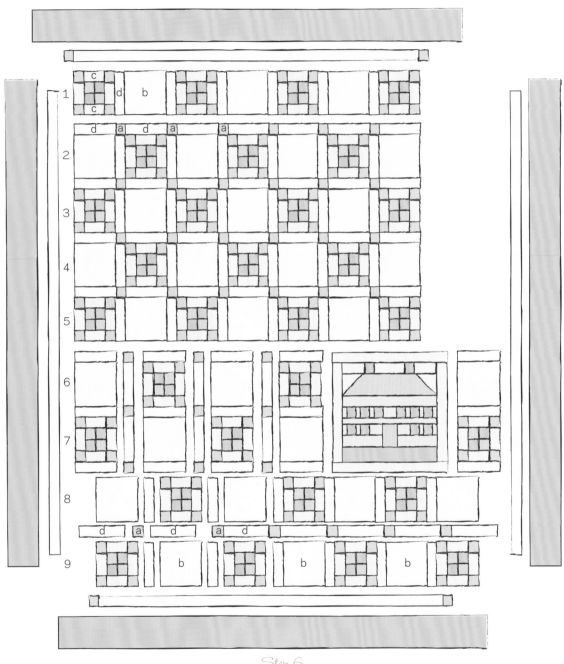

Step 6

Second variation of Fresh Vintage Patchwork is shown here along with our featured quilt. Titled "Summer Throw," this version shows a completely different use of color placement, thus changing the appearance of the patchwork significantly. I love that color can do that! For these instructions, visit www.figtreequilts.typepad.com.

About the Author

Joanna Figueroa is a beloved fabric designer, pattern designer, active quilt instructor, and owner of the respected Fig Tree & Company. She has earned a loyal fan base as a licensed fabric designer for MODA FABRICS for the past seven years, releasing several best-selling collections each year. She is currently working on her 24th collection in her signature *Fresh Vintage™* style.

Joanna owns and operates Fig Tree & Company alongside her husband, Eric, her right-hand man in all their business endeavors. Fig Tree offers a fresh perspective on traditional quilting and sewing patterns, focusing on quilts, whimsical kids' items, home furnishings, and personal accessories. Fig Tree offers more than 150 stand-alone patterns, several self-published booklets, and a quarterly magazine called *Fresh Vintage*, and operates a thriving wholesale business to more than 800 stores worldwide. Joanna's work is regularly shown at shops, quilt shows, and retreats throughout the United States, Europe, and Australia.

She is a regular contributor to numerous publications, such as *American Patchwork & Quilting*, *Quilts & More*, *American Quilt Retailer*, and *Quiltmania*. Her work and studio have been featured in various books and magazines, including *The Quiltmakers*, *Les Edicion de Saxe*, *Australian Patchwork & Quilting*, *Where Women Create*, and *The Book of Inspiration*.

At Joanna's website, www.figtreeandcompany.com, you can peruse her designs, browse her online shop, or sign up for her online newsletter. To follow her design adventures, stop by her popular blog, Fresh Figs, at www.figtreequilts.typepad.com or follow her on twitter at figtreeandco.

Joanna lives in the San Francisco Bay Area with her husband, three kids, their neurotic beagle, Lucy, and "Fishie," the goldfish with nine lives.